THE RICKENBACKER BOOK

TONY BACON & PAUL DAY

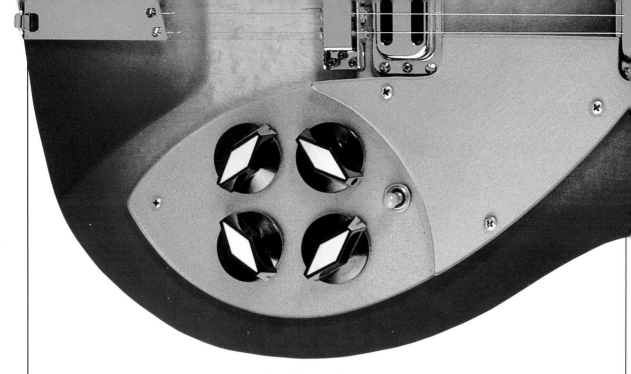

The Rickenbacker Book
A complete history of Rickenbacker electric guitars
By Tony Bacon & Paul Day

GPI Books
An imprint of Miller Freeman Books, San Francisco

Published in the UK by Balafon Books, an imprint of Outline Press Ltd,
115J Cleveland Street, London W1P 5PN, England.

First American Edition 1994
Published in the United States by Miller Freeman Books,
600 Harrison Street, San Francisco, CA 94107
Publishers of GPI Books and *Guitar Player* magazine
A member of the United Newspapers Group

ISBN 0-87930-329-8

Library of Congress Catalog Card Number 94-71408

Printed in Hong Kong

Art Director: Nigel Osborne
Design: Sally Stockwell
Editor: Roger Cooper
Typesetting by Type Technique, London
Print and origination by Regent Publishing Services

94 95 96 97 98 5 4 3 2 1

CONTENTS

INTRODUCTION

In the 1930s, Rickenbacker made some of the earliest electric guitars ever put into production, and this book tells the full story from those trail-blazing days right up to the most recent instruments manufactured by the contemporary California-based company.

We describe how Swiss immigrant Adolph Rickenbacker met the inspired guitarist/inventor George Beauchamp, and chart the gradual rise of Rickenbacker's instruments.

In the early 1950s Adolph sold his guitar-making operation to California businessman Francis Hall, and we analyze how Hall brought the company up to date and launched the new designs that established the modern Rickenbacker operation. The popularity of the company's guitars took an enormous leap when The Beatles used them in the 1960s, and we track Rickenbacker's progress from then until today's artist 'signature' guitars, intriguing new instruments, and reissues of classic models.

New interviews with leading Rickenbacker personnel both past and present inform our story (which does not include basses or acoustic guitars). Throughout the book we present dozens of specially commissioned full-color photographs of fine guitars, many from Rickenbacker's exclusive collection.

A comprehensive reference section completes the book, designed to overcome the confusion that many players and collectors experience when trying to identify Rickenbackers. You will find concise dating information, and detailed listings of every Rickenbacker electric guitar issued from 1932 to 1994. If you're fascinated by guitars in general, or love Rickenbackers in particular, we feel sure that you will enjoy our fresh look at this unique, stylish guitar maker.

TONY BACON & PAUL DAY, ENGLAND, APRIL 1994

"I now use my Rickenbacker 12-string more than anything else. It's a great guitar, you can get so many sounds from it. It's like experimenting with an organ."

George Harrison *TALKING IN 1964 ABOUT A NEW AND INSPIRING INSTRUMENT*

"The Rickenbacker 12-string with the aid of electronic compression gave us the distinctive 'jingle jangle' sound that we would later be known for."

Roger McGuinn *ON THE GUITAR THAT SHAPED THE SOUND OF THE BYRDS IN THE 1960s*

"I'm quite surprised now that Rickenbacker are happy to have me sponsor an instrument which is so tied up with such an anarchic part of my career. It's the only guitar I've ever sponsored... and I've done it partly out of guilt."

Pete Townshend *ON HIS COMPLETELY UN-SMASHED RICKENBACKER 'SIGNATURE' GUITAR OF 1987*

"The first attraction was the look, because I liked Pete Townshend on the early Who stuff. When I got an advance from the record company I went and bought as many Rickenbackers as I could."

Paul Weller *ON HOW THE PUNK BOOM OF THE 1970s HIT RICKENBACKER SUPPLIES*

"I'm essentially a rhythm player, and you can do that with a Rickenbacker. It's not really a lead instrument, it's more of a rhythm guitarist's kind of thing."

Tom Petty *UNDERLINES THE CLASSIC ROLE OF THE RICKENBACKER*

"It was George Harrison who influenced me to get a Rickenbacker: 'Ticket To Ride' – what a brilliant song!"

Johnny Marr *ADMITS WHO PUT THE JANGLE INTO THE SMITHS IN THE 1980s*

"When I first started playing I used to buy by color: what do you have in black guitars? They'd pull out five and I'd pick one out. I was just lucky enough to stumble on a Rickenbacker."

Peter Buck *OF REM RECALLS A FORTUITIOUS CHANCE MEETING*

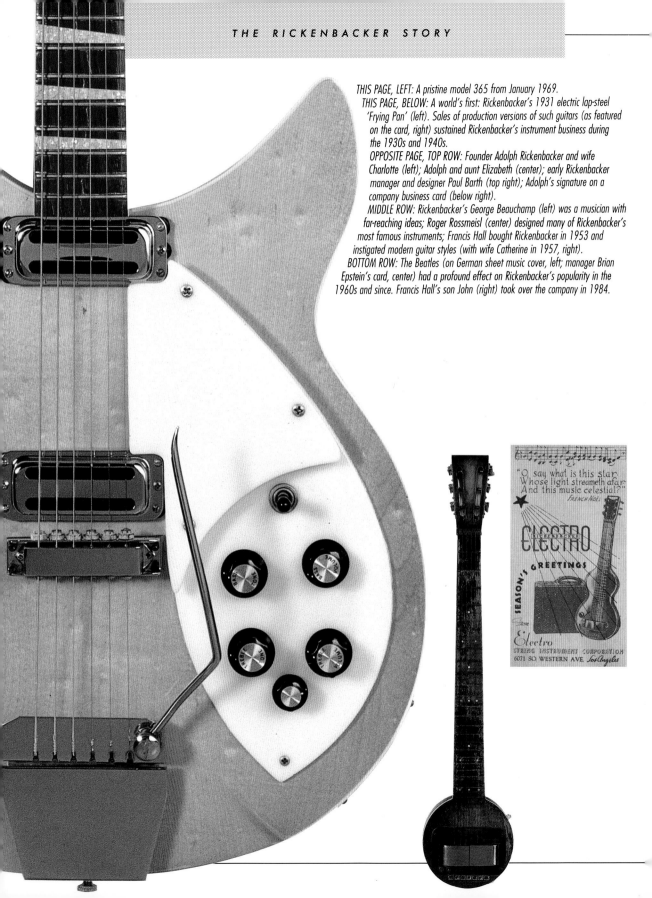

THIS PAGE, LEFT: A pristine model 365 from January 1969.

THIS PAGE, BELOW: A world's first: Rickenbacker's 1931 electric lap-steel 'Frying Pan' (left). Sales of production versions of such guitars (as featured on the card, right) sustained Rickenbacker's instrument business during the 1930s and 1940s.

OPPOSITE PAGE, TOP ROW: Founder Adolph Rickenbacker and wife Charlotte (left); Adolph and aunt Elizabeth (center); early Rickenbacker manager and designer Paul Barth (top right); Adolph's signature on a company business card (below right).

MIDDLE ROW: Rickenbacker's George Beauchamp (left) was a musician with far-reaching ideas; Roger Rossmeisl (center) designed many of Rickenbacker's most famous instruments; Francis Hall bought Rickenbacker in 1953 and instigated modern guitar styles (with wife Catherine in 1957, right).

BOTTOM ROW: The Beatles (on German sheet music cover, left; manager Brian Epstein's card, center) had a profound effect on Rickenbacker's popularity in the 1960s and since. Francis Hall's son John (right) took over the company in 1984.

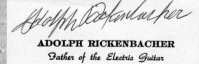

ADOLPH RICKENBACHER

Father of the Electric Guitar

(714) 525-0176   1801 VISTA LOMITAS DR.
FULLERTON, CALIF.

DIE BEATLES

In Ihrem großen United-Artists-Film-Erfolg

Yeah Yeah Yeah

(A HARD DAY'S NIGHT)

ROLF BUDDE MUSIKVERLAGE, BERLIN

Brian Epstein,

Managing Director.

Nems Enterprises Ltd.

24, Moorfields, Liverpool, 2.   *Central 0793.*

THE STORY of Rickenbacker guitars starts before the beginning of the 20th century, with a man named Adolph Rickenbacker. He was born near Basel, Switzerland, in April 1886, but while still young was brought to the United States and lived with members of his family in Ohio, later moving to Illinois. A cousin of Adolph's was Eddie Rickenbacker, born in Columbus, Ohio, who became a fighter pilot in the US 94th Pursuit Squadron during the 1914-18 World War I. Eddie shot down 27 German aircraft, a feat which earned him the coveted title 'ace of aces.'

In about 1918 Adolph finally moved to Los Angeles, California, and in the 1920s established a successful tool-and-die operation there, stamping out metal and plastic parts to customers' requirements. It's possible that Adolph may have offered these facilities to help cousin Eddie with his ill-fated attempt to manufacture Rickenbacker automobiles in the 1920s. Generally, however, Adolph did very well from the tool-and-die business, and his wealth was also boosted when he married Charlotte, a native of Pennsylvania who seems to have been rich through family oil business connections.

In the late 1920s, work for guitar makers formed a profitable strand of the Rickenbacker Manufacturing Company's operations. One especially enthusiastic customer for metal parts was the National String Instrument Corporation, based usefully close by Rickenbacker's premises in Los Angeles.

National had begun their activities in the late 1920s, specializing in the production of the 'ampliphonic resonator' acoustic guitar. This used the novel idea of suspending resonating aluminium cones inside a metal body as the basis for a series of loud, distinctive instruments. Adolph Rickenbacker had bought stock in National as a result of their business dealings – Rickenbacker's shop made the metal bodies and resonator cones for National – and Adolph was even nominally pictured as company Engineer in some of National's publicity leaflets at the time.

Depending on which of the many conflicting stories one believes, National's resonator guitar principle was invented either by John Dopyera or by George Beauchamp – and more likely a combination of the two. Dopyera was originally an instrument repairer who went on to team up with various of his brothers over the years to manufacture National and also later Dobro guitars.

Beauchamp was a Texas-born vaudeville guitarist and a keen tinkerer who had moved to Los Angeles. Adolph Rickenbacker wrote later in a short history of his early business activities about George's departure from Texas: "His pappy gave him a mule and an old wagon and told him to 'git,' and that is about all he had with the exception of an old guitar. Things were pretty tough those days for the guitar player, as the guitar was not loud enough to be heard in a band or orchestra. George got to using his head, as that was about the only thing he had left, besides his pretty wife."

Like many performers in the 1920s, Beauchamp was fascinated by the potential for increasing the loudness of conventional flat-top and archtop acoustic guitars. Ensemble playing demanded more volume than such guitars could reasonably offer, and apparent mechanical solutions such as National's loud resonator instruments began to appear.

Some stories suggest that Beauchamp had originally approached John Dopyera with a request to fit a peculiar horn attachment to a guitar in order to increase its volume. Dopyera complied – but from that transaction followed the rather more practical resonator scheme. Author and musician Bob Brozman, who has documented the National story in a recent book, described George Beauchamp as "the catalyst for John Dopyera's radical ideas."

BEAUCHAMP'S PICKUP

Beauchamp became General Manager at National, but was apparently still not content with the extra volume afforded by the National guitars' principle of mechanical resonators. He started to wonder about the possibility of electric amplification – and once again he was not alone. Across the United States, and elsewhere too, players were experimenting with early – and crude – methods of amplifying their instruments, some by sticking record-player pickups into acoustic guitars and playing them through the device's amplifier and loudspeaker, still others by meddling with microphones.

Another potential solution was a magnetic pickup designed

especially for guitars, and this was the goal at which Beauchamp aimed. As Adolph noted in his later account: "[George] had better ideas. If you can amplify radio waves, why not amplify vibration waves?"

Helped by fellow National employee Paul Barth (a nephew of the Dopyeras), Beauchamp began to put together a basic magnetic pickup system for a guitar. Household gadgetry once again proved useful in this regard: George Beauchamp used his washing machine's motor to wind the coils for the pickup, and as his son Nolan told *Guitar Player* magazine in 1974: "My uncle had a Brunswick phonograph, and my father took the pickup out, extended the wires, and mounted it on a two-by-four [block of wood] with a single string. That's how he first proved that his theory was practical. He then began perfecting his six-string pickup."

LUCKY HORSESHOE

The theory of the electro-magnetic pickup is quite straightforward. Of course, as with most breakthroughs, it was Beauchamp's application of a seemingly simple idea to a specific use that was inspired. A 1930s Rickenbacker leaflet has a handy description: "Without going deeply into a technical detail, let us briefly explain how it works. A metal string vibrating before the poles of a magnet disturbs the field of magnetic force, and the sound waves are translated into electrical energy. These electric waves are then passed on to the [amplifier] enormously augmented, and by means of a speaker delivered to the listener once more as sound waves. A rheostat provides perfect volume control. Sounds simple, doesn't it? Yet the inventor worked many weary months to perfect the device."

Beauchamp's experiments had culminated in a pickup consisting of a pair of horseshoe-shaped magnets that enclosed the pickup coil and effectively surrounded the strings. When Beauchamp and Barth had a working version, probably around mid-1931, they roped in yet another National man, Harry Watson, to build a one-piece maple 'lap steel' guitar on which to mount the prototype pickup. Nolan Beauchamp again: "Harry came over one day and made it by hand with a wood rasp, a hand coping saw and a couple of clamps on an old beat-up bench in the back of our garage." This was the famous wooden 'Frying Pan' guitar, so-called because of its small round body and long neck (see photograph, page 6). It was the first to feature an electro-magnetic pickup, and in that sense the basis for virtually all modern electric guitars.

Beauchamp, Barth and Adolph Rickenbacker teamed up to put the ideas of this exciting prototype electric guitar into production. They formed the curiously named Ro-Pat-In company, together with a couple of other individuals, at the end of 1931 – just before Beauchamp and Barth were fired by National during a shake-up of that organization. No doubt the events were not coincidental.

In 1933 and 1934 Beauchamp filed applications for a patent for what is now generally referred to as the 'horseshoe' pickup. The patent was eventually granted to him in August 1937, and had already been assigned to the company by an agreement dated December 1935. It was not unusual for patents to take this long to proceed through the system. Adolph said in a private 1960s interview that it was only because of a demonstration in front of the patent administrators that they were finally convinced of the pickup's viability: "The patent office wouldn't give us a patent because they didn't think it was feasible. So we sent I think it was [musicians] Danny Stewart, Dick McIntyre and Sol Hoopii to Washington to play for about 15 minutes before the patent attorneys. It was only a few days before we got notice that our patent would be issued."

FRYING PAN PRODUCTION

In summer 1932 Ro-Pat-In started manufacturing cast aluminum production versions of the Frying Pan electric lap-steel guitar, complete with horseshoe electro-magnetic pickups. These guitars are now recognized to be of great historical importance because, while other makers such as Acousti-Lectric (later Vivi-Tone), National, Dobro, Stromberg-Voisinet (later Kay), Epiphone and Gibson experimented in the 1930s with electric guitars, Ro-Pat-In's Frying Pans were effectively the first electric guitars put into general production. Some of the better-known companies mentioned above were also producing mainly acoustic instruments, based on many years of experience, but the upstart Ro-Pat-In made only electric guitars.

9

The Sweethearts Of The Air
(right) This mid-1930s trio adopt a
happy playing pose with their
Rickenbacker electrics – a lap-steel
(center) and more unusually, an Electro
Spanish model (right).

KEN ROBERTS' Model Spanish Guitar

★ This Rickenbacker Electro Spanish Guitar is very popular with
the artists. The neck is joined to the body at the seventeenth
fret, which permits a player to jump from one octave to another and
to work-in many different effects on higher notes. The body is the
regular concert size, made from three ply mahogany finished in two-
tone brown, light in the center and dark toward the edges, which are
celluloid bound. A handsome, entrancing instrument. Price, complete
with speaker, $110.00. Price of Guitar alone, $87.10.

Rickenbacker catalog c1935
(left) The cover of this early edition
boldly proclaimed 'Brother Musician
Listen To A Miracle'. Included in this
modest entreaty was the Ken Roberts
acoustic-electric, with a Kauffman-
designed vibrato tailpiece.

Spanish (SP) c1948 (above)
Launched in 1946, this was to be the
final non-cutaway Rickenbacker archtop
electric to appear. It featured unusually
placed f-holes, as found on the earliest

Rickenbacker of this type, the Electro
Spanish. Like that model, the neck and
body of the SP model were supplied by
the Harmony instrument making
company of Chicago.

Electro Spanish c1936 (above) This variant of Rickenbacker's lap-steel was introduced in 1935, the first of its type to be designed as a conventional guitar. Featuring the same all-bakelite construction, it also shared the lap steel's mini-sized, semi-solid body, but now with the neck joining at the 14th fret. The guitar pictured is an early example with a single control – later versions came with two. The Kauffman vibrato tailpiece was an option.

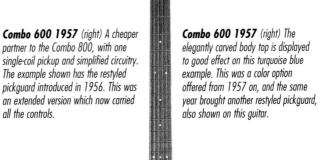

Vibrola Spanish (above) A variation of the Electro Spanish with a deeper body to accommodate the unique motor-powered vibrato system devised by C O 'Doc' Kauffman, this novel guitar was very heavy and came with a necessary stand as well as accompanying amplifier.

Combo 600 1957 (right) A cheaper partner to the Combo 800, with one single-coil pickup and simplified circuitry. The example shown has the restyled pickguard introduced in 1956. This was an extended version which now carried all the controls.

Combo 600 1957 (right) The elegantly carved body top is displayed to good effect on this turquoise blue example. This was a color option offered from 1957 on, and the same year brought another restyled pickguard, also shown on this guitar.

Combo 800 1955 (right) The first 'proper' Rickenbacker six-string electric, appearing in 1954, the Combo 800 initially used a single 'Multiple Unit' pickup which had two coils, designed to individually enhance bass and treble response.

11

Early examples of the Frying Pans tend to have an 'Electro' brandname on the headstock, and as they are designed for the lap-steel or Hawaiian style of playing, where the player rests the guitar on the knees and slides a steel bar over the strings, they are usually referred to by players and collectors as the Electro Hawaiian models.

By 1934 the Rickenbacker name – or to be more precise 'Rickenbacher' – had been added to the headstock logo. Adolph always used the original, and as far as he was concerned correct, un-anglicized version spelled with an 'h' rather than a second 'k.' At first this was the way it appeared in the brochures and on the guitars with the new Electro Rickenbacher brandname, but later the familiar Rickenbacker spelling was adopted. A Rickenbacker family historian has suggested that the change was made by some members of the family because of nervousness about misinterpretation of Germanic associations during the World Wars. Also in 1934, the name of the manufacturing company was changed from the bizarre Ro-Pat-In to the much more logical Electro String Instrument Corporation.

FRYING PANS STICK

Despite their ground-breaking status, the early Electro and Electro Rickenbacher aluminum electric lap-steels did not sell in spectacular numbers. Probably little more than a dozen Hawaiian electrics were sold in 1932, a poor record not helped by the depressed economic conditions of the time and the relative scarcity of general electricity supplies.

Adolph wrote later: "The really difficult part was selling them and getting players to use them. Everywhere we would go they just would not have anything to do with the instrument. All the bands were afraid to use it in the fear that [an amplifier tube] would go in the middle of a number.

"We were finally allowed to demonstrate one on a stage show – that was our big moment! After setting it up and the player began to play, all at once the speaker of our amplifier announced 'KHJ Los Angeles' [a local radio station broadcast]. The manager pulled the cord and practically threw us out! But George did not give up – he licked that trouble. But we still could not get anyone to play the electric guitar. After about two

years of hard work and spending about $150,000, we were ready to give up."

Also around this time, Electro produced some 'Spanish' wood-bodied electric guitars – that is, guitars played in the 'traditional' fashion, as opposed to the lap-steels. The first, the Electro Spanish, appeared around 1932 – among the earliest of its kind – and the Ken Roberts model, named after a session guitarist, followed about three years later. These and other similar models consisted of 'conventional' wooden acoustic guitar shells bought in by Electro from companies such as Harmony or Kay (both prolific guitar makers based over in Chicago) and fitted with Electro's distinctive horseshoe pickup at the company's Los Angeles workshop. "Think of the orchestral possibilities," suggested Electro's publicity. It seems that few players did; these wooden Spanish electrics apparently sold in very small numbers.

Aluminum turned out to be an unsuitable choice of material for the early Electro lap-steels. It would expand in hot conditions, especially under stage lights, and regularly conspired to put the guitars out of tune. So Electro looked for a better material – and hit on Bakelite. Later they also made lap-steels from stamped sheet metal.

BEAUTIFUL BAKELITE

Bakelite was the first synthetic plastic – a hard, tough, heatproof phenolic resin invented by Belgian-American chemist Leo Baekeland in 1909, and popularized in the 1930s for many household objects. Adolph had already had experience with Bakelite in his tool-and-die business, making plastic toothbrushes among other items, and Electro produced guitars using the material after having obtained a license from an Englishman, Arthur Primrose Young, who had been granted a patent in 1932 whichg covered the production of molded musical instrument necks and bodies.

As we are primarily concerned in this book with the history of Rickenbacker's electric Spanish guitars, the move to Bakelite was crucial. In 1935 Electro produced its first guitars made from the material, the Model B Hawaiian lap-steel version, and the Electro Spanish version (later also called the Model B). The usual differences between Hawaiian and Spanish versions were present, the Hawaiian type featuring a higher string action and the typical 'squared' neck cross-section. A further difference was that the neck joined the body at the 10th fret on the Hawaiian and at the 14th on the Spanish version.

The Bakelite Spanish was arguably the first 'solidbody' electric guitar. In fact the small, waisted Bakelite body was semi-solid, but the tiny pockets under the thick, solid top were intended to reduce weight rather than to add any acoustic resonance to the instrument.

"What would you say of a Hawaiian guitar you could hear a quarter of a mile away on a clear day, or a Spanish guitar louder than any piano?" trumpeted an Electro publicity leaflet of the 1930s. "That's what we have in the new Rickenbacher Electro instruments." While the Spanish Bakelite model did not sell well, the Hawaiian versions greatly improved Electro's position, both in the United States and in various export markets. They took off in the late-1930s, and are still regarded today as especially fine lap-steel guitars. It's worth noting that at this time the Electro guitar factory, based at South Western Avenue, Los Angeles, was run by George Beauchamp, while Adolph Rickenbacker oversaw the tool-and-die business in the other half of the building. So it is fair to assume that the introduction of the Bakelite models was, once again, the responsibility of Beauchamp.

However, after only a few years Beauchamp apparently began to tire of the guitar business. In 1940 he sold his share interest and left Electro, reportedly to set up an operation to market fishing equipment, but died very shortly afterwards. George Beauchamp, one of the great innovators of the modern electric guitar, was gone forever.

In his later account, Adolph summed up his feelings about the modest growth of Electro during the Depression era of the 1930s: "As I sit here writing this, I just happened to think – the doctor told me to get lots of rest and go to bed early. And as I go to sleep listening to some good Hawaiian music, I feel proud of George and myself that we did not let the guitar players down. And I don't know of any other thing that has ever happened to put so many boys back to work!"

It was in the late 1930s that Clayton 'Doc' Kauffman came to the attention of Electro. Doc, originally from Kansas, was a lap-steel guitarist, violinist and relentless tinkerer who became famous for his brief but crucial association with Leo Fender in the K&F company of the 1940s (K&F = Kauffman and Fender) before the Fender name was well known.

DOC AND THE VIBROLA

The first of Doc's inventions to be used by Electro was his vibrato unit, among the first hand-operated guitar-mounted devices for changing the strings' pitch and inducing vibrato effects (commonly but erroneously called 'tremolo' by many players and guitar makers).

Kauffman reportedly came up with his 'Vibrola' in the late 1920s, and his eventual patent is dated January 1932. The unit was crude and fragile, working with a sideways motion, in the same direction as the player's picking hand. To activate the unit its arm was pulled up and a simple hinge let the tailpiece forward, flattening the strings. When the arm was released a small spring (theoretically) returned the tailpiece to its original position. Electro made an exclusive licensing agreement with Doc in February 1936 to "manufacture, use and vend the said invention for all fretted musical instruments" for an initial period of five years.

Electro used it first on the Ken Roberts model, and on various other Electro and Rickenbacker instruments until about 1960 – of which more later. Rather more bizarre was Kauffman's patented motorized vibrato system, which the company built into their Vibrola Spanish guitar, introduced at the very end of 1936. Another of Electro's wonderfully over-the-top press announcements proclaimed the new model as "the most outstanding improvement in the Spanish guitar since the Moors brought the instrument from the Far East to Spain about the year 1088 AD."

Powered by an electric motor, the contraption was fitted inside a modified Bakelite electric Spanish model. An arrangement of belt-driven arms and axles activated a Vibrola unit, giving an automatic and constant vibrato effect designed to emulate Doc's beloved violin sound. This additional ironmongery resulted in a guitar even heavier than the standard Bakelite model, and it had to be supported by a stand (see pictures on pages 3 and 11)

13

Model 1000 1957 (right) The cheapest in a trio of short-scale 'student' solids introduced in 1957. As with the high-end versions, these beginners' Rickenbackers employed through-neck construction. However, unlike its partner 900 and 950 models, the 1000 came with 18 frets instead of 21, and the resultant shorter neck necessitated a different body styling, akin to the more pronounced tulip shape found on the 400 and 450.

Combo 450 1957 (above) This two pickup version of the Combo 400 was launched in 1957. The outward curving horns provide the 'tulip' shape of these models. The through-neck section is clearly visible at the body end, beyond the gold-anodized metal pickguard carrying two 'oven'-style control knobs which Rickenbacker had introduced in the mid-1950s.

Rickenbacker catalog 1956 (left) The cover commemorates the 25th anniversary of Rickenbacker's first electric guitar, the lap steel Frying Pan prototype (see photo page 6).

CELEBRATES ITS 25th YEAR IN
ELECTRIC GUITARS · AMPLIFIERS · CASES AND ACCESSORIES

Rickenbacker catalog 1957 (right) This page shows the Model 900 and 950. It illustrates the differences in body styling between these and the 18-fret 1000. The two 21-fret guitars have a much shallower left cutaway, the thicker horn joining the neck at the 13th fret.

Model 1000 1964 (above) In late-1957 styling of the cheaper models was revised. The right cutaway became more shallow as the result of a slight inward curve.

Combo 450 (above) This example from Rickenbacker's collection is missing a tuner, and we felt it unwise to alter this rare guitar for our photograph.

Jean 'Toots' Thielemans (left) Shown on the cover of Accordian & Guitar World, this Belgian-born guitarist performed with the George Shearing Quintet. As a Rickenbacker endorsee he proved instrumental in John Lennon's choice of guitar during the Beatles' early years.

Combo 400 1956 (above) Appearing in 1956, the Combo 400 was a slab-bodied, through-neck solid, priced below the carved-top Combo 600 and 800. It was the first to feature the new tulip-shape body styling. The anodized metal pickguard carried one single-coil bar-magnet pickup.

Doc had worked on prototypes in his Fullerton workshop, using parts bought from Electro. At first he tried wood bodies but moved on to Bakelite. Among the first of a very limited number of customers for this strange instrument was Perry Botkin, described by Electro as the "famed radio star" who "supports singing stars such as Al Jolson, Eddie Cantor, Bing Crosby and others." Botkin bought the first experimental version for $150, and Electro used his picture in advertising materials. In an agreement dated October 1937 and signed by Botkin and George Beauchamp, Electro said it would "exchange one of the first finished models for the experimental guitar and continue to supply him with improved instruments from time to time."

At the end of 1938 Botkin wrote to Kauffman about the 'Vibratar' (an alternative name for the Vibrola Spanish): "I have a definite idea about an improvement... it has to do with keeping it in tune when you don't use the vibrato. Stop in a music store that sells Brunswick records and listen to a record I made several weeks ago, 'Hong Kong Blues' with Hoagy Carmichael. I use the Vibratar without the vibrato. No one seems to know just what is going on. Several people have asked me about it since the record was released." Kauffman had modified both his own and Botkin's Vibrola Spanish with a switch to turn the vibrato effect on and off, rectifying the original's basic flaw of being on all the time. But the whole project was switched off soon afterwards, and very few Vibrola Spanish models were actually sold. Electric guitars were unusual; this one was plain weird. We can only guess that Adolph would have been thankful that his tool-and-die business was successful enough to finance the losses that such guitar projects must surely have been incurring at this time.

Paul Barth, still with the company, received a patent for a version of the 'horseshoe' pickup designed as a separate add-on item for acoustic guitars, and also used on Electro's S59 archtop wood-bodied electric. After Beauchamp's departure from Electro in 1940 Barth assumed wider responsibilities and became factory manager after World War II. In summer 1942 Electro stopped making musical instruments to begin production for the war effort, and Adolph said later that it made vacuum control valves among other things.

During these years that the company was working for the government it managed to extend the Los Angeles factory premises. Early in 1946, after World War II was over, the company got back to some semblance of normal business. However, Adolph decided not to reinstate many of the musical instrument lines that had been running before the war, including most of the poorly received Spanish styles. A lone exception was another wood-bodied electric, actually called the Spanish (or sometimes 'SP'). But Adolph's heart appears no longer to have been in the electric Spanish guitar business. During 1946 he had turned 60, and given later events we can assume that around this time Adolph began to think about selling the musical instrument part of his operation.

ADOLPH SELLS UP

Francis Cary Hall was born in Avon, Iowa, in September 1908, and moved with his family to California when he was around 11 years old. In high school he studied radio and electronics, and this became Hall's great interest, leading to him owning only the second radio set in Orange County, south Los Angeles (his instructor had the first).

In his teens, Hall began a tentative money-making scheme by recharging the big batteries that radio sets required and, having spotted a demand, had started a business to manufacture them by the late 1920s. This operation developed into a radio repair store, Hall's Radio Service, and that led logically to a wholesale company that distributed electronic parts, the Radio & Television Equipment Co (often shortened to R&TEC or, as we shall call it, Radio-Tel), which Hall set up in Santa Ana, Orange County, in 1936.

One of Radio-Tel's customers was another Orange County-based radio repair store, Fender Radio Service, run by Leo Fender in Fullerton, some 15 miles from Santa Ana. Leo had set up the K&F company with Doc Kauffman and the two had started to make electric lap-steel guitars and small amplifiers toward the end of 1945. In 1946, just after Leo and Doc ceased working together, Radio-Tel became exclusive distributors for the new Fender Electric Instrument Co, selling the electric lap-steels and amps with this new brand.

By 1953, with the Fender Telecaster electric solidbody guitar and Fender Precision electric bass in production, Fender's business had begun to pick up, and the existing sales arrangement with Radio-Tel was re-organized into the new Fender Sales company, based like Radio-Tel in Santa Ana and with four business partners: Leo Fender; Francis Hall; Don Randall (general manager of Radio-Tel); and Charlie Hayes (a Radio-Tel salesman).

Later that year, Francis Hall (generally known as F.C. Hall) began to see the potential for running a musical instrument business where he not only distributed the product, but also manufactured it. "I understood that Adolph Rickenbacker was interested in selling his instrument corporation," recalls Hall, "which I was told about through another person. Adolph's main interest was in the tool-and-die business, not the musical instruments."

So in late 1953 Hall bought the Electro String Music Corporation from Adolph. An agreement dated December 7th and signed by Adolph Rickenbacker (Electro president), Charlotte Rickenbacker (Electro assistant secretary) and F.C. Hall stated that the purchase was complete, and that without any further payment Electro could continue indefinitely "to use the trade name 'Rickenbacker' in connection with the advertising and selling of all said electric guitars."

HALL AND FENDER

For a couple of years Hall continued his association with Fender Sales. It would appear that his experience gained in association with Fender and his general view of the guitar business at the time led Hall to consider that the way forward for Electro might well lie in the production of electric Spanish-style guitars. The lap-steel business was still reasonably good, based primarily on guitar schools whose students were encouraged to move on to better models as their skills improved. But in the early 1950s it appeared that the instrument's popularity had passed its peak, and so Hall began to set his sights on fresh targets for the newly acquired Rickenbacker business.

The guitar factory was still at South Western Avenue, Los Angeles, and Hall recalls that there were around six employees when he bought it, including factory manager Paul Barth,

producing "a small quantity" of electric lap-steel guitars and amplifiers. Adolph Rickenbacker's tool-and-die business remained in the other half of the building. Radio-Tel's headquarters had always been in Santa Ana, and in 1956 moved from Oak Street to better premises on South Main Street.

ROSSMEISL ARRIVES

Around the beginning of 1954 Paul Barth hired Roger Rossmeisl to work for Electro. Rossmeisl was born in 1927 near Kiel in the Schleswig Holstein region of northern Germany. His father, Wenzel Rossmeisl, played jazz guitar and started to build guitars in about 1935, using the brand Roger, named after his son. After World War II the Rossmeisls moved east to Berlin, opening a workshop there, and the teenage Roger began to learn about guitar-making. Shortly afterwards Wenzel established another workshop much further south while Roger remained in Berlin. 'Roger' electric models appeared by 1947; five years later Roger Rossmeisl decided to emigrate to the United States.

Ted McCarty, president of the prestigious Gibson company in Michigan, says that he received a letter from Rossmeisl asking if he could come to the United States and work for Gibson. "He was supposedly a master guitar maker, had a certificate from somebody in Germany," remembers McCarty somewhat disdainfully. "But anyway, I brought him over here, paid his fare to come to work in our factory. He stayed about a year and left." McCarty says that Rossmeisl didn't get on too well with his fellow workers, many of whom were of Dutch descent and still felt animosity toward Germans so recently after the end of World War II, especially one like Rossmeisl with his halting English.

"He wanted to make a guitar like a Gibson L-5," McCarty continues, "but *his* way, the way *we* should have. So we let him do it. I swear, the top was real thick, and clumsy... you could have used it as a bat," he laughs. Maybe somewhere there exists a Gibson Rossmeisl one-off guitar? "Anyway," McCarty continues, "after Rossmeisl left Gibson he went on vacation, and he got a job playing guitar on a ship going to Hawaii. Then he came back to Los Angeles. We never saw him again."

Roger Rossmeisl joined Electro after his Hawaiian

18

Susanna Hoffs (above) A long-time Rickenbacker fan, and in 1988, while lead singer with all-girl group The Bangles, Hoffs enjoyed the privilege of a signature model. This was based on the 350 Liverpool guitar, and a limited edition of 250 was made.

325S/1966 1964 (left) The f-hole and black knobs identify this guitar as an export version of the 325 made primarily for the British market, where John Lennon's use of a similar model was used in its marketing (see 1965 'Beatle backer' ad, below). The 325, sporting three 'toaster top' pickups and vibrato tailpiece, had been the flagship of a new series introduced in 1958. It employed 'sweeping crescent' styling on a small semi-solid body, and its unusually short-scale neck felt even smaller thanks to a significantly slimmed-down shape. After Lennon adopted the model it was assured lasting fame – regardless of the odd feel of that short neck.

Combo 850 1957 (above) This guitar, and partner Combo 650, was the first to feature the new 'sweeping crescent' body styling in 1957. Apart from the revised shape, all else was very similar to the existing Combo 800. In late 1957 an additional pickup was fitted at the neck, as on this example.

John Lennon's *original 325 and 325/12. Lennon acquired his first 325 (right) in Hamburg in 1960. Although he had the guitar refinished in black in 1962, it has since been returned to its natural color, along with the addition of a white pickguard (originally gold) and new knobs. Lennon added the Bigsby vibrato tailpiece and bridge soon after he got the 325, and used it as his main stage and studio guitar with The Beatles from 1960 to early 1964. The 325/12 (left) was a one-off non-standard model made specially for Lennon by Rickenbacker in February 1964, but its ungainly combination of 12 strings on a short-scale neck meant that Lennon rarely used the guitar.*

John Lennon's *second 325 (right) During the Beatles' first visit to the US in 1964 Rickenbacker gave Lennon this most famous of 325s, as a replacement for his original. It had a new vibrato (the arm is damaged here) and revised five-knob control layout. Lennon immediately began using the guitar regularly with his group, and is seen playing it on this 1960s magazine cover (below).*

ENTER FOR THE AMPLIFIER COMPETITION INSIDE

BEAT INSTRUMENTAL

MONTHLY JAN. 1966 No. 21

DRUMMERS' ARGUMENT

ANIMALS found GOLDIE

AMPLIFIER BUYING

NORTH WEST BEAT

19

John Lennon's Rickenbackers
This remarkable and unique collection, shown for the first time in a book, consists of the two guitars that John Lennon used on all the classic Beatles concerts and records, along with a one-off 12-string made specially for him by Rickenbacker in 1964.
When Lennon went to play in Hamburg with The Beatles in 1960 he took his cheap Höfner electric guitar with him, but while there he managed to obtain the natural-finish Rickenbacker 325

(above), and used the guitar with The Beatles for a little over three years. The black 325 (right) became Lennon's favorite from early 1964, and is the guitar that most people associate with his Beatles live performances. Lennon also used this guitar widely for recording, including a number of tracks for albums such as A Hard Day's Night, Help! and Rubber Soul.
It is likely that these three instruments are among the most valuable electric guitars in the world.

adventure, probably early in 1954, and it's likely that Paul Barth hired him with the specific intention of having him work on new designs for Rickenbacker electric guitars. Rossmeisl's skills were evidently improving rapidly.

COMBO TIME

That same year the Electro company launched their first 'modern' electric guitars, the Combo 600 (listed in the fall 1954 pricelist at $229.50) and the Combo 800 (at $279.50). In a sense, these first Combo models were aptly named, combining the horseshoe pickup and almost square neck of the earlier Hawaiian lap-steels with the up-and-coming solid electric Spanish approach. Rossmeisl must surely have seen the new Gibson Les Paul model solidbody electric, launched in 1952, before he left Gibson, and there are some elements of that instrument in the Combo design (see the photos on page 11).

It seems likely that the design of these first Combo models was shared between Rossmeisl, F.C. Hall and Paul Barth. Hall says that he designed the control circuits, and that Rossmeisl was "one of the engineers involved," probably contributing the physical aspects of neck and body. Barth may well have been responsible for the more mechanical components, such as the new guitars' bridges.

These initial Combo models of 1954 shared the same general styling: a carved-top body with two cutaways – the lower gently pointed, the upper more bulky. Some of the bodies were fully solid, but others had the beginnings of a construction feature that with later modifications became typical of Rickenbacker: the back of the solid body would be partially scooped out to reduce weight, and in these particular examples the back was then covered with a plate. Some necks were bolted on, others glued.

At first the 600 and the 800 each had a single horseshoe pickup, although the 800 used one with double coils (the Rickenbacker catalog of the time calls it a 'Multiple-unit'). These were in fact an early kind of humbucking pickup. Later versions of the 800 have two separate pickups: a horseshoe unit near the bridge and a more conventional looking 'bar'-type closer to the neck.

The first Combo models began to feature a brand new 'underlined' Rickenbacker logo on their headstocks, of the type still used by the company today. John Hall, the current owner of Rickenbacker, says that his mother, Lydia Catherine Hall (wife of F.C. Hall), designed the logo and the distinctive curved, pointed plate on which it appears. "She just got out her scissors and cut shapes out of paper and figured it out. It's a great logo, visible at 100 yards, there's no question as to what it is." The lettering style is typical of the 1950s, and the interlinked characters recall contemporary automobile logos that were designed as one continuous strip of chrome.

The new Rickenbacker logo emphasized the fresh importance of this sole brandname for the company's guitars. Hall saw that solid-type Spanish electrics were the way forward: "I thought the new style guitar would be more practical," he recalls, "and would create more sales volume." It didn't at first: the Combo guitars were slow sellers, and the guitars must have been a small part of Hall's overall Radio-Tel business at the time. Novelties were tried: for example, some of the early Rickenbackers have a circular metal plate on the back of the body with a fitting for a saxophone-style carrying strap. This did not last.

Gradually Rickenbacker became more adept at making their new designs appealing to musicians. The company's next move was to abandon the clumsy horseshoe pickup and apply a more suitable type to their Spanish electrics, in keeping with the designs used by other electric guitar makers of the time such as Gibson, Kay, Fender, Harmony and Gretsch. First model to receive the new pickup was the Combo 400, launched in 1956 at $174.50. The 400 was also the first Rickenbacker with a new body shape, generally referred to now as the 'tulip' style because of its outwardly curving cutaways. Another first was a through-neck, a feature that would become a familiar aspect of many of Rickenbacker's solidbody guitars.

As the name implies, a through-neck guitar has a neck which is not bolted or glued to the body, as is usual, but which extends right through the length of the instrument, with 'wings' attached either side to complete the full body shape. A supposed benefit of such a design is that the strings and their associated bridge, tailpiece, nut and tuners are all located on the same piece of wood, enhancing sustain and tonal resonance. The through-neck design of Rickenbacker's Combo 400 of 1956 had few precedents, although one notable example was the historic Bigsby/Travis guitar, an early solidbody electric built by engineer Paul Bigsby in the late 1940s for country musician Merle Travis.

Also in 1956, Radio-Tel stressed the longevity of the Rickenbacker name by promoting the 25th Anniversary of the Frying Pan electric. "Twenty-five years ago the world first heard the music of the electric guitar," proclaimed one of the anniversary brochures. "It was the creation of the Electro String Instrument Corporation, manufacturers of Rickenbacker Electric Guitars. The introduction of this electronically amplified music launched a new era in the entertainment field."

END OF FENDER

F.C. Hall's relationship with the Fender Sales company ended in 1955. The connection must surely have become difficult as Rickenbacker's competing guitars began to hit the market. Charlie Hayes, one of the four partners of the Fender Sales company, was killed in a car accident in 1955, and there seems to have been disagreement among the other three as to how to continue the partnership. "Francis [F.C. Hall] bought the Rickenbacker company," says partner Don Randall, "so we bought his interests in Fender Sales, which became Leo and myself." Hall says: "When Charlie was killed I decided that I would also turn in my stock. Randall and Fender handled the sale of it, settled on that basis."

At least one of Radio-Tel's customers was well behind such news. A dealer from Arizona tried to order Fender equipment from Radio-Tel in October 1957, and F.C. Hall wrote back politely informing him that Radio-Tel had not distributed Fender gear for more than four years. As a good businessman, Hall also took the opportunity to explain the virtues of Rickenbacker guitars, concentrating on the twin-pickup Model 950, one of three new short-scale models that Rickenbacker had released that year (the other two being the single-pickup Model 900 and Model 1000).

At first the 'three-quarter-scale' 900 and 950 had appeared with a slightly revised version of the outwardly curving tulip

body shape, but later in the year Rickenbacker gave them a new shape with an inward-curving lower cutaway, as Hall explained in his letter to the Arizona dealer. "This guitar has the body cut in such a way that the 21st fret can be reached very easily, and chords can be played in the highest fret positions," he said. "This feature was added after the picture was taken for our catalogues, but all instruments which are now shipped will have this added feature." Thus Rickenbacker offered the full-scale Combo 400 in the revised shape, and also added the Combo 450 as a new model for 1957, effectively a two-pickup version of the 400.

SWEEPING CRESCENT

Of much greater importance to Rickenbacker's long-term guitar designs was a pair of models introduced in 1957, the Combo 650 and Combo 850. These guitars introduced a body shape that in various incarnations and dimensions has been in continual use by Rickenbacker right up to the present day. The 650 and 850 were small-body guitars, and the elegant body style is distinguished by a sweeping crescent-shaped curve across the two cutaways (take a look at the examples pictured on pages 18 and 19).

Rickenbacker referred to this new shape in a press release as the "new extreme cutaway body, permitting all frets on the slender neck to be reached with equal ease." The 650 and 850 were also among the first to contain Rickenbacker's new double truss-rod system for correcting neck movement. In theory, here was a more adjustable set-up, although it has been the result of much confusion among players and repairers over the years, many of whom misunderstood the operation of the rods. A few even discovered a new Rickenbacker feature as a result of their misinformed manipulations, the pop-off fingerboard, while some induced neck cracks after tampering with the truss-rods. Rickenbacker eventually simplified the truss-rod system in 1984.

By July 1957, Rickenbacker's pricelist could boast a respectable lineup of nine electric Spanish models: the Combo 850 at $279.50 (in turquoise blue; a natural maple option cost $289.50); the Combo 800 at $279.50 (blond or turquoise blue); the Combo 650 $217.50 (turquoise blue; natural at $227.50);

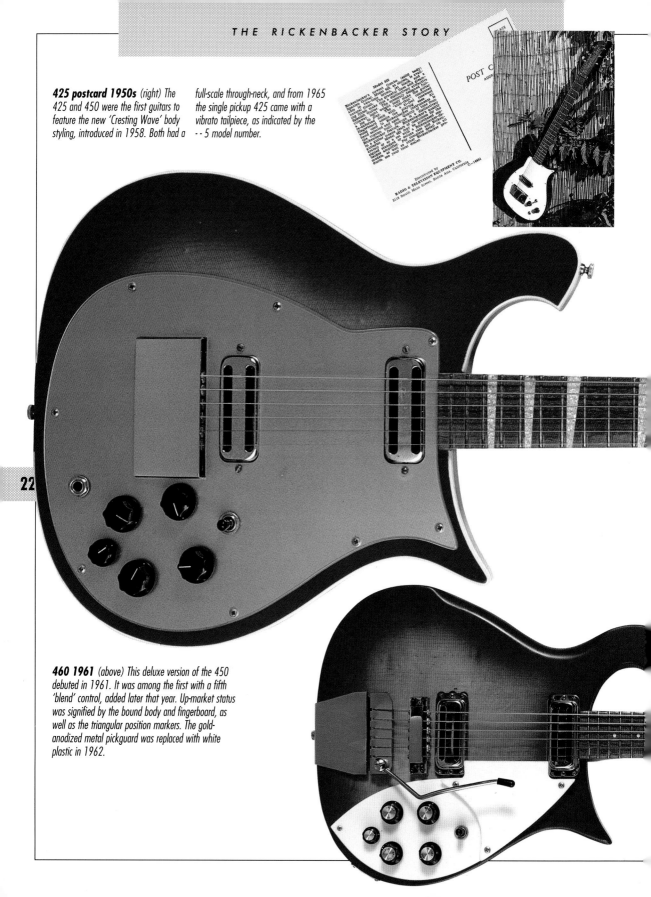

425 postcard 1950s (right) The 425 and 450 were the first guitars to feature the new 'Cresting Wave' body styling, introduced in 1958. Both had a full-scale through-neck, and from 1965 the single pickup 425 came with a vibrato tailpiece, as indicated by the - - 5 model number.

460 1961 (above) This deluxe version of the 450 debuted in 1961. It was among the first with a fifth 'blend' control, added later that year. Up-market status was signified by the bound body and fingerboard, as well as the triangular position markers. The gold-anodized metal pickguard was replaced with white plastic in 1962.

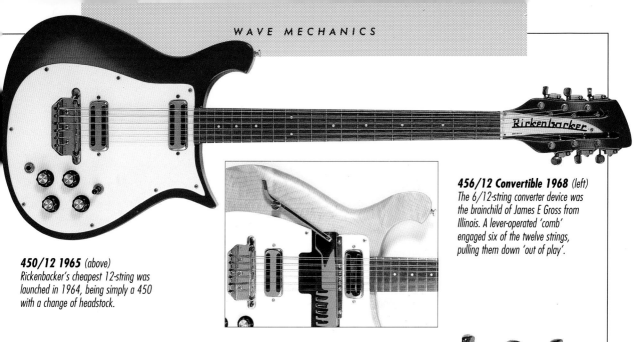

450/12 1965 (above)
Rickenbacker's cheapest 12-string was launched in 1964, being simply a 450 with a change of headstock.

456/12 Convertible 1968 (left)
The 6/12-string converter device was the brainchild of James E Gross from Illinois. A lever-operated 'comb' engaged six of the twelve strings, pulling them down 'out of play'.

23

615 1967 (above) This model shared the same hardware as the more ornate 625, including twin pickups and new Ac'cent vibrato tailpiece. Earliest examples of both guitars came with a single layer gold plastic pickguard carrying four controls; this is the later white/5-knob type.

625 1967 (above) Two new models were added to the Rickenbacker electric range of early 1962, the 615 and 625. The latter was the more expensive, its triangle position markers plus binding on body and fingerboard being the established indicators of deluxe status. By 1963 both guitars came with a pickguard with a separate, raised section, in white plastic – a two-tier assembly that has become a distinctive feature on many Rickenbacker instruments.

Combo 600 $229.50 (blond or turquoise blue); Combo 450 $179.50 (jet black, cloverfield green or montezuma brown); Combo 400 $159.50 (colors as 450); Model 950 $149.50; Model 900 $114.50; and the Model 1000 at $104.50 (last three all jet black).

Around this time Paul Barth left Rickenbacker, going on to work in various small guitar-making operations, including his own Barth company in the late 1950s as well as Bartell and Magnatone in the 1960s. At Rickenbacker, Barth was replaced as factory manager by Ward Deaton, who headed up a team of around a dozen workers at Rickenbacker's Los Angeles factory, including foreman Bill Myers. Roger Rossmeisl continued as 'chief designer' (although official job titles did not exist) and had a number of assistants working under him, including Semie Moseley who came and went in the late 1950s. Moseley later set up his Mosrite company, best known for the Ventures model guitar as played by that top 1960s instrumental group. It had some design features that recall the work of Rossmeisl. Another of Rossmeisl's assistants then was Dick Burke, who joined Rickenbacker in March 1958. At the time of writing Burke is still with Rickenbacker, as factory manager, and thus qualifies as their longest-standing employee.

Towards the end of 1958 Rickenbacker brought out two new solid models with a new body shape. The single-pickup 425 ($149.50) and twin-pickup 450 ($184.50) had a body that brandished a hooked upper horn, lending the guitar the appearance of a 'cresting wave' shape across the two cutaways. Over the years this style has been used on a variety of Rickenbacker solid electrics, and is still used today.

STARTING THE CAPRI

As it turned out, 1958 was an exceptionally important year for Rickenbacker. It was in '58 that a series of new models was introduced that formed the basis for Rickenbacker's success during the 1960s.

These thin hollow-body electric guitar designs – known at first as the Capri series, and named after the Hall family's cat – were largely the responsibility of Roger Rossmeisl. Of course, Rossmeisl reacted primarily to direction given by his superiors at Rickenbacker, as Dick Burke recalls. "If Mr Hall wanted

something, Roger would try to come up with it," he says. "First off, he'd usually put a small sketch of it on paper." But Rossmeisl does seem to have been something of a loner, happier when working in isolation on a new design, and trying to do most of the jobs himself rather than delegating tasks to others. Another Rickenbacker man comments that Rossmeisl was, for those reasons, probably not best suited to the teamwork that a production environment often demands, but that his talent for design could balance out any such shortcomings.

For the new electric hollow-body Capri guitars, more accurately described as 'semi-acoustics,' Rossmeisl further developed the scooped-out construction principle that had first been used on some of the early Combo models. Rather than make a hollow guitar in the traditional acoustic method – where a flat, carved or pressed top is secured to a back and rims – the Capri models were built from a solid block of wood, usually two halves of maple joined together. In simple terms, this was cut to a rough body shape, and then *partially* hollowed out from the back. A separate wooden back was then added once all the electric fittings had been secured, and the neck was glued into place. It's certainly unusual – and to this day it remains pure Rickenbacker methodology.

THE LITTLE ONE

The first such Capri model to be announced by Rickenbacker was the small-bodied 325 model, a guitar that would have a great effect on the company's success when it was taken up a few years later by John Lennon.

F.C. Hall regularly sent out General Sales Bulletins to Radio-Tel's salesmen to keep them up to date with new product developments. In one such Bulletin dated February 1958, Hall previewed the 325 model, "the first item in the Capri series hollow-body guitars."

Hall continued: "Others have made combination models of acoustic and electric... our model is made strictly as an electric guitar, but has all the qualities of the solid-body models.

"The hollow-body has definite advantages in many respects over solid-body electric guitars. First of all, it is lighter in weight which makes it easier to handle – it only weighs 5¼ pounds. It is thicker so it looks more like an acoustic guitar.

Also, the body is two inches longer than the bodies used on our Model 900 and 1000 series. The body on the new model measures 16 x 13 x 2 inches.

"The bodies and necks are attractively finished in a natural finish similar to our Combo 850... We are also introducing for the first time a brown two-toned finish, sometimes called 'Sunburst,' which adds considerable class to the appearance of the guitar for those who wish a darker finish...

"Furthermore we have made this model with the three-quarter neck which many professionals feel is much easier to play than the standard conventional length neck. Also it is easier for a student or a person with a small hand to play the new model as the fingering is closer together."

The point about pro players and the short-scale neck did not turn out generally to be the case. Quite simply, the cramped confines of short-scale guitars make them harder to play by those with full-scale hands. Hall went on to mention the 325's three chrome-plated pickups, its "famous" Kauffman vibrato unit (with a cautionary note about the danger of detuning the strings through extreme use) and the guitar's "full cutaway" for access to the 21st fret. Hall's note to his salesmen concluded by quoting a list price for the forthcoming Capri 325 of "only $249.50 without the case. I am sure you will not find another guitar with all of these features, precision balanced, near this price," he said.

Another Rickenbacker feature highlighted by the Capri models was a very slim neck, achieved in combination with the company's double truss-rod system, and later Rickenbacker's distinctively glossy, lacquered fingerboard was added. These models also began to appear with two now-classic Rickenbacker design elements: 'toaster-top' pickups (nicknamed after their split chrome look); and two-tier pickguards, at first in an arresting gold-colored plastic. These split units had a base plate flush to the guitar's body carrying the controls, and a separate pickguard raised on three short pillars, intended to act as a finger-rest.

Later in February 1958 a further General Sales Bulletin from F.C. Hall made the first mention of "full length Capri guitars." Hall told his salesmen that this style of instrument, a full-size version of the small-bodied 325 type, "will be available at least as a sample to you some time in April". He predicted, deadpan and, as it turned out, dead accurately, "It will be a very popular guitar."

The full 12-model Capri Series lineup was detailed on Rickenbacker's June 1958 pricelist, under three headings. *Three-quarter necks:* 310 $224.50 (two pickups, two-tone brown or natural finish); 315 $239.50 (as 310 but with vibrato); 320 $239.50 (as 310 but three pickups); and 325 $249.50 (as 310 but three pickups and vibrato).

Full-necks: 330 $259.50 (two pickups, two-tone brown or natural finish); 335 $274.50 (as 330 but with vibrato); 340 $274.50 (as 330 but three pickups); 345 $289.50 (as 330 but three pickups and vibrato).

Deluxe full-necks: 360 $309.50 (two pickups, two-tone brown with white binding or natural with brown binding, triangle-shaped fingerboard inlays); 365 $329.50 (as 360 but with vibrato); 370 $329.50 (as 360 but three pickups); 375 $348.50 (as 360 but three pickups and vibrato).

The July 1958 issue of *Music Trades* magazine publicly announced the 12-model Capri range, due to be launched to dealers at the National Association of Music Merchants (NAMM) trade show that summer.

KNOBS AND KAUFFMANS

Some of the hardware used on the original Capris increased the idiosyncratic air of these guitars, most notably Rickenbacker's distinctive control knobs with diamond-shaped pointers on top. These large knobs looked equally at home on kitchen ovens of the period – hence their subsequent nickname. The vibrato-equipped models were fitted with the quirky Kauffman units, which remained awkward and flimsy and with a distinct tendency to render the strings out-of-tune after even delicate use... but they did at least look different.

The distinctive appearance of the Capri guitars was curvaceous and stylish (see the examples on page 30), a testament to the design sense of the German-born Rossmeisl. In fact some of the apparently new elements seem more familiar when considered in the context of contemporary German guitar design – especially the wonderful scimitar-shaped (nicknamed 'slash') soundhole with which most of the

660/12TP Tom Petty 1993
(left) In 1991 Rickenbacker added another signature model, the Tom Petty 12-string. This limited edition of 1000 has many special features including: black/white 'checker' body binding, 12-saddle bridge, vintage-style hardware, gold plastic two-tier pickguard and a wider neck. The latter appeals to those who find Rickenbacker's standard 12-string spacing too narrow.

620 1988 (left) The triangular position markers together with the bound fingerboard and body confirm that this is a deluxe specification instrument. A non-vibrato version of the 625, it was introduced in 1977 as a replacement for both that model and the more basic 615. This example presents an unusual 'albino' appearance, provided by the combined effect of white body, neck and the matching white plastic two-tier pickguard.

Tom Petty (above) The man proudly holding a fireglo finished example of his signature 12-string.

460 1965 (left) The 460 underwent some changes to components as well as cosmetics during the early 1960s. The fifth 'blend' control became standard by late 1961, and a white plastic pickguard was substituted for the gold-anodized metal type during the following year. The early 1960s also saw Rick-O-Sound stereo circuitry fitted as standard, rather than a special order option.

650S Sierra 1993 (right) In the early 1990s Rickenbacker launched two brand new instruments, namely the 650A Atlantis and 650E Excalibur. These were joined by further versions including the 650S Sierra. All feature a plated metal pickguard and 24-fret, wider dimensioned through-neck. The all-maple construction of the latter provides a distinctive appearance.

600 Series catalog 1993 (above) Previous Rickenbacker literature has been somewhat inconsistent in terms of design and content. The current system conveniently divides the range into different series, with an appropriate full color brochure for each, providing more than adequate coverage and information on the relevant models.

27

Capri models were equipped, the triangular fingerboard inlay on 'deluxe' models, and the elegant recess carved in the front of the body to accommodate the tailpiece.

Also during 1958, Rickenbacker added a Thick Body model to the full-scale Capri series, featuring a lavishly carved, deep body. Here again Roger Rossmeisl's German heritage was evident, and in fact the raised 'shoulder' running parallel to the edge of the body on these guitars (see pages 38-39) is generally referred to as a 'German carve,' a typical feature of the work of some German guitar-makers, including Roger and his father Wenzel. Despite detailing 14 different electric and acoustic Thick Body models on the July 1958 pricelist, Rickenbacker in fact only produced one 'German carve' electric model, the two-pickup 381, which sold for $498.

As if all this wasn't enough, early in 1959 Rickenbacker launched yet another addition to the Capri range. If anything, the Thin Full-Body series was rather more conventional than 1958's newcomers. These guitars were 'thin' in cross-section, like the 310-375 Capri models, but their 'full' body was larger in outline (see page 42) and boasted a single rounded cutaway that recalled the type seen on some other guitars of the period, for example a number of Gibson's contemporary ES models.

Rickenbacker gave these Thin Full-Body models an F suffix, and they first appeared on the company's April 1959 pricelist. Dick Burke recalls that there were some problems with body cracks on the 'F' instruments, and indeed production appears to have been relatively modest. The pricelist notes that the guitars were officially available in the standard two-tone brown or natural finishes, as follows: 330F $249.50 (two pickups); 335F $274.50 (as 330F but with vibrato); 340F $274.50 (three pickups); 345F $289.50 (as 340F but with vibrato); 360F $299 (two pickups, bound body and neck, triangle-shaped fingerboard inlays); 365F $329.50 (as 360F but with vibrato); 370F $329.50 (three pickups, bound body and neck, triangle-shaped fingerboard inlays); 375F $348.50 (as 370F but with vibrato).

Die Beatles in Deutschland

In Liverpool, England, a fledgling three-man guitar 'group' of great ambition if little activity gradually evolved during the course of 1960, dropping their original name of The Quarry Men and after a number of variations on the theme deciding to call themselves The Beatles. They added a bass player and then a drummer to the original trio, and in August their almost-but-not-quite manager Allan Williams achieved the rather remarkable feat of securing the under-rehearsed group a run of no less than 48 nights at the Indra club in Hamburg, northern Germany.

The Beatles took their basic instruments and equipment with them for what turned out to be a grueling engagement. George Harrison had an unlikely-sounding Neoton Grazioso, a cheap Czech-made guitar rather better known by its later name of Futurama. Bassist Stuart Sutcliffe struggled with a big German Hîfner 500/5 bass, while Paul McCartney, still a guitarist at this stage of the group's career, played an undistinguished Dutch-made Rosetti-branded Solid 7 model. John Lennon got by on a £28 Hîfner Club 40 electric hollow-body guitar.

Lennon's First Rick

While in Hamburg, Lennon acquired a Rickenbacker Capri 325, which must have looked magnificent compared to the guitars that the group were used to. "I sold my Hîfner, made a profit on it too, and bought one," Lennon told *Beat Monthly* magazine a few years later. "It's the most beautiful guitar, the action is really ridiculously low."

George Harrison remembers going to a music store in Hamburg with Lennon to buy the guitar, and that it was the first Rickenbacker he'd ever seen. Harrison (as well as Rickenbacker) reckons that Lennon bought the 325 from the Steinway music store in Hamburg, although local research suggests that the guitar may have been acquired from the nearby Musikhaus Rotthoff.

"I bought a Gibson amplifier and John bought that little Rickenbacker," Harrison recently recalled on BBC Radio 1. "I think he'd just seen an album by Jean Thielemans, who used to be guitar player in the George Shearing Quintet and had one of those Rickenbackers." Some reports suggest that Lennon actually saw Jean 'Toots' Thielemans playing a Rickenbacker in Hamburg — certainly the Belgian guitarist/harmonica-player did play in Germany in 1960, probably with Kurt Edelhagen's radio orchestra among others.

Whichever Hamburg shop window it was hanging in, that good quality U.S.-made Rickenbacker 325 was, Harrison confirms, an almost unbelievable sight to the pair of raw Liverpudlian musicians. "You have to imagine that in those days, when we were first out of Liverpool, any good American guitar looked sensational to us. We only had beat-up, crummy guitars at that stage. We still didn't really have any money to buy them, but I remember that John got that Rickenbacker and I got this amplifier. And we got them what they call 'on the knocker,' you know? [Money] down and the rest when they catch you! I don't know if we ever really paid them off," he laughed.

There are suggestions that Lennon may have ordered the Rickenbacker specially, but Harrison recalled: "I think it was purely because John needed a decent guitar, and that one happened to be in the shop and he liked the look of it."

Lennon's prized Rickenbacker 325, probably a 1958 or 1959 model, was finished in natural maple, and at first had the standard 'oven' knobs and Kauffman vibrato... but neither of these fixtures were apparently to Lennon's liking. The knobs he replaced quickly with smaller Höfner types, while the Kauffman gave way to a more efficient Bigsby vibrato unit.

Guitarist Chris Huston of fellow Liverpudlian band The Undertakers had a factory-fitted Bigsby vibrato unit on the Gibson guitar he used in 1960, which Huston remembers today as "the first Bigsby in Liverpool." He recalls: "John and I were pretty good friends, and not too long after he came back with the Rickenbacker we went into Hessy's music store in Liverpool, and he bought a Bigsby unit from salesman Jim Gretty. John had his guitar with him, and we put it on the counter, unscrewed the old vibrato, which obviously wasn't as good, and screwed on the Bigsby."

OUT IN THE FIELD

Meanwhile, back in California, the Rickenbacker team had their hands full with the new semi-acoustic line (no longer called Capri after 1959) as well as the solidbody lines. Salesman Joe Talbot remembers some of the efforts being made

to market these new Rickenbacker guitars to the music store owners around the country. Talbot worked as southern-states salesman for Rickenbacker between 1959 and 1961, having been introduced to F.C. Hall by the well known steel guitarist Jerry Byrd, a long-standing Rickenbacker devotee.

Talbot remembers taking to the road with a Capri 365 and a Rickenbacker amplifier to demonstrate the new line to his customers in Texas, Oklahoma, Tennessee and the surrounding states. "I only called on larger towns, because the smaller towns had maybe one music store with all the big lines, and didn't have any necessity for a new line," Talbot recalls. "But in the bigger towns you could find a music store that did not have all the well known lines and might have a need for another line of guitars and amplifiers.

"Most of them thought the 365 was a beautiful, gorgeous guitar. First time or two around I'm not sure that they were sold. It was kind of new to them, though people did know Rickenbacker – they were better known then for the Hawaiian guitars. But this time around Rickenbacker had this gorgeous, new, very complete line, from small solidbodies right up to big hollow-bodies. I had a full catalog with pictures of everything and a brief description. The dealers' attitude wasn't negative, it was more, 'Well, let me wait and see.'

"If the store had someone in it that was a guitar player, they would compare the 365 to the other guitars they had. Those that did not play evaluated it more on its appearance – and it was impressive!"

Talbot says that he perceived the competition at that time to come primarily from Fender – "that sound that everybody was after" – and also mentions that Gibson's new thinline semi-acoustic electric launched in 1958, the ES-335, while selling very well, was not seen by the music stores that he visited around 1960 as such a direct competitor for Rickenbacker's guitars.

Back at the factory some modifications were being made to the guitar lines. From about 1960 the existing two-tone brown sunburst finish was officially called autumnglo, and a new red-to-yellow sunburst option began to appear, officially named fireglo. A reliable new serial-numbering system was established in 1960 (explained in the reference section at the

330 1958 (left) The 'sweeping crescent' body profile was used on both small and large-sized electrics, all initially marketed under the Capri model name. The 330 was the first thin, full-size hollow-body, debuting in 1958. Early examples encompassed many cosmetic and hardware variations.

360 1959 (below) Following a logical styling pattern that would become established Rickenbacker practice, the 360 was a deluxe version of the 330, with obvious cosmetic differences. The body was bound, likewise the fingerboard, which also sported triangular position markers.

Fast Play Neck ad 1960s (above) This extolled the virtues of Rickenbacker's 21-fret neck with 'easier, faster reach'.

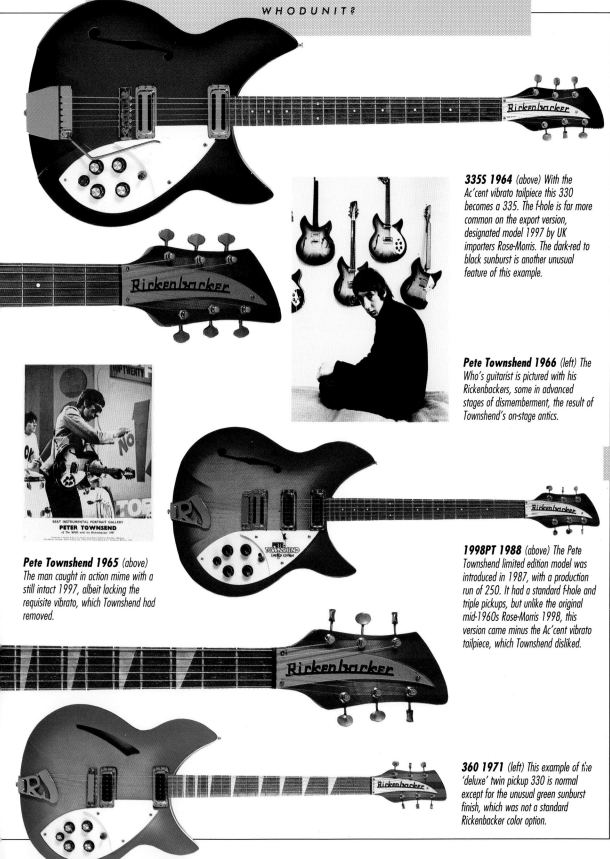

335S 1964 (above) With the Ac'cent vibrato tailpiece this 330 becomes a 335. The f-hole is far more common on the export version, designated model 1997 by UK importers Rose-Morris. The dark-red to black sunburst is another unusual feature of this example.

Pete Townshend 1966 (left) The Who's guitarist is pictured with his Rickenbackers, some in advanced stages of dismemberment, the result of Townshend's on-stage antics.

Pete Townshend 1965 (above) The man caught in action mime with a still intact 1997, albeit lacking the requisite vibrato, which Townshend had removed.

1998PT 1988 (above) The Pete Townshend limited edition model was introduced in 1987, with a production run of 250. It had a standard f-hole and triple pickups, but unlike the original mid-1960s Rose-Morris 1998, this version came minus the Ac'cent vibrato tailpiece, which Townshend disliked.

360 1971 (left) This example of the 'deluxe' twin pickup 330 is normal except for the unusual green sunburst finish, which was not a standard Rickenbacker color option.

31

back of this book) and a new stereo output feature called Rick-O-Sound was added to some guitars, usually the 'deluxe' models, from around the summer of that year.

Rick-O-Sound exploited the new interest at the time in stereophonic sound, consolidated in 1958 when most of the big recording companies began issuing stereo records. At this time Gretsch and then Gibson launched 'stereo' guitars, and Rickenbacker decided to follow suit. The company's system simply separated the output from neck and bridge pickups so that a special split cord would feed the individual signals to two amplifiers (or to two channels of one amplifier).

This pseudo-stereo feature was made possible by a special double jack socket plate fitted to Rick-O-Sound-equipped Rickenbackers. One socket was marked 'Standard': when an ordinary mono jack plug was inserted here, a switch contact inside disconnected the stereo circuit and provided normal guitar output.

The 'Rick-O-Sound' socket required a stereo plug connected to a 'Y' cord. Rickenbacker offered this as an accessory with an interconnection box, rather grandly called the Rick-O-Sound Kit, for $24.50 (it first appeared on the July 1960 pricelist).

In many cases, guitars with Rick-O-Sound were simply used in mono, and the extra facility ignored. Salesman Joe Talbot recalls Rick-O-Sound's introduction in 1960, and says, "I frankly don't remember there being that much response to it, simply because it required more investment – you had to have two amplifiers."

A DIFFERENT ACCENT

It was also around this time that Rickenbacker decided to replace the unpredictable Kauffman vibrato with a new unit, the Ac'cent. Although by no means a sophisticated or especially sturdy vibrato, it was at least an improvement on the Kauffman. The Ac'cent uses a sprung steel plate attached to a tailpiece section. Pressure on a bent metal arm affects spring tension, providing the vibrato effect.

Rickenbacker salesman Joe Talbot remembers coming across a sample of the Ac'cent in a music store in Texas, probably some time in 1960, and writing to F.C. Hall about this

potential replacement for the problematic Kauffman. Talbot was getting complaints about the old vibrato from his customers: "People found it hard to keep the guitar in tune with that earlier one – it drove me crazy!" So next time Talbot was at the Rickenbacker headquarters in Santa Ana, he and Hall traveled to San Diego to see the maker of the Ac'cent units, and Hall soon completed a deal for Rickenbacker to use them on their guitars, beginning around 1961. The earliest units have "Ac'cent By Paul" on the steel plate, and as well as employing them on vibrato models like the 325 and 335 Rickenbacker offered Ac'cents as add-on accessories for $42.50 each (first noted on the July 1961 pricelist). There is strong evidence to suggest that the Ac'cent was made by exactly the same manufacturer who produced Gibson's similar Maestro Vibrola unit during the 1960s.

Another new vibrato was tried on a few Rickenbackers a year or so later. Called the Boyd Vibe and apparently devised by Solon Boyd and/or Marvin Boyd (the latter of whom worked for Rickenbacker at the time) it was of poor design and didn't appear on many instruments nor for very long. Solon Boyd subsequently tried to market the Boyd Vibe separately, but even with an enthusiastic endorsement from country guitarist Merle Travis it enjoyed little success.

In 1961 Rickenbacker introduced a deluxe guitar with the same body shape as the earlier 425, 450 and vibrato-equipped 615 and 625 models. The new 460 ($248.50) had triangle-shaped fingerboard markers, Rickenbacker's most obvious indicator of a deluxe model, but more significantly was the first to carry a modified control layout of a type that the company would apply to nearly all their models over the next few years. On the 460 a fifth 'blend' control was added, situated just behind the four normal controls and fitted with a smaller knob. The extra control seems to have been prompted by an idea that F.C. Hall had about tone circuits.

The fifth 'blend' knob is much misunderstood by guitarists, and it must be said that its effect can be very subtle. Consider the usual control set-up for a two-pickup guitar: there are individual volume and tone controls for each pickup, and a selector switch. The three-way selector offers either: (1) the pickup nearest the neck, with a more bassy tone often used for rhythm playing; (2) both pickups, balanced by the relative positions of the two volume controls; or (3) the pickup nearest the bridge, with a more treble tone for lead playing. Rickenbacker uses this control system too, but from 1961 started to add the fifth knob to many models.

The theory is that in the neck-pickup-only or bridge-pickup-only position on the three-way selector, the fifth knob gives the opportunity to blend in some tone from the *unselected* pickup. For example, if you just had the bassier neck pickup selected, the fifth knob would allow you effectively to blend in a little of the bridge pickup's treble tone.

If the selector is in the middle position – in other words, giving both pickups – then the fifth knob allows you to vary the precise balance between the two, for increased tonal emphasis. In fact, the later development of modern channel-switching amplifiers made the fifth knob redundant, but at the time it did seem to Rickenbacker to offer some increased versatility to the available tones.

On Rickenbackers fitted with the Rick-O-Sound stereo feature, the fifth knob functions more as a balance control between left and right (ie neck pickup and bridge pickup), because the selector would usually be lodged in the center position so that both pickups are 'on.'

Confused? You are not alone. Musicians have generally found the fifth 'blend' knob rather baffling, and no doubt many quickly decided to forget that their guitar had a fifth knob. Beatle George Harrison sounded as exasperated as many when he spoke of his confusion: "That tiny little knob never seemed to do anything," he told BBC Radio 1 in 1987. "All it ever seemed to be was that there was one sound that I could get where it was bright, which was the sound I used, and another tone where it all went muffled, which I never used."

L.A. TO SANTA ANA

Back in 1962, The Beatles had begun their rise to fame. John Lennon was still using his Hamburg-bought Rickenbacker 325 model, and after some damage to the natural-colored guitar Lennon had it refinished black, possibly in October 1962. No doubt unaware at this stage of John Lennon and his 325, a British distributor of musical

instruments, Rose-Morris, had written to Rickenbacker in July to enquire about selling the California company's products in the U.K.

Rickenbacker had been involved in some export business, but for the moment did little to follow up this particular proposal. The company was busy that summer moving the factory from South Western Avenue, Los Angeles – where Rickenbacker guitars had been made since the 1930s – down to Kilson Drive, Santa Ana, not far from the Radio-Tel headquarters. The regular shifting of new guitars some 35 miles from Los Angeles to the distribution center in Santa Ana was becoming tiresome, especially for F.C. Hall's wife, Catherine, who generally took charge of such business. "And I lived in Orange County," F.C. recalls, "so the move consolidated things, and cut down some of the overheads."

Dick Burke, who'd worked for the company for four years, also remembers welcoming the move in 1962. "I wanted to get out of L.A.," he says. "Santa Ana was real small at that time, there were no freeways about, and I liked the country. I think we had about the same factory space at the new place, but the actual buildings were bigger."

ROSSMEISL DEPARTS

Most of the dozen or so workers stayed on after the move south, but soon afterwards Roger Rossmeisl left the company and went to work for Fender in Fullerton (about 15 miles away), hired primarily to work on a new line of acoustic guitars. More than any other single person, it was Rossmeisl who created the classic Rickenbacker look, and despite his sometimes unorthodox methods, Rossmeisl's departure must have been a blow to the company. Burke says that Rossmeisl was already planning to leave when the factory was moved, and had by that stage bought a new house nearer to the Fender plant. Rossmeisl stayed at Fender until about 1968. He eventually returned to his native Germany, and died there in 1979 aged only 52.

Rickenbacker's July 1962 pricelist showed the current line-up of no less than 32 electric models, split into four types, as follows. *Combo Series, Solid Bodies:* 425 $179.50; 450 $249.50; 460 $299; 625 $359.50; 950 $169.50; 900 $139.50;

1993 1964 (left) The 1993 was a UK-market export version of the 330/12, but with double-bound body and f-hole.

Convertible Guitars (above) This 1966 flyer promotes the new 366/12 and 456/12 Convertibles with a great deal of enthusiasm and misplaced optimism.

Rose-Morris (above) This April 1964 catalog shows the range offered in the UK at the time.

360/12V64 1993 (above) This reissue appeared 20 years after an original was presented to The Beatles' George Harrison in 1964. The current production item has the same cosmetics, including 'slash' soundhole and trapeze tailpiece. Harrison is pictured (left) with his very early 360/12 in a 1960s Beat Instrumental. The 1964 hotel message (far left) heralds the meeting between The Beatles and Rickenbacker in February, when the 12-string became Harrison's.

336/12 Convertible 1967 (above) This jetglo finished 330/12 carries a 6/12 Converter unit, logically becoming the third member of the Convertible trio.

34

ALSO NEW:

599.⁰⁰

The Model 331 combines a fine musical instrument with the thrill of a
lightshow. Internally lighted by a
set of frequency modulated lamps,
this instrument will shimmer with
infinite color and pattern variety.
The three modulation channels are
controlled by a sensitivity control
to make this patented instrument
a beautiful performer in the stage
situations professionals encounter.

331 leaflet c1970 (above)
Rickenbacker's contribution to
psychedelia was promoted in a low-key
fashion with this flyer.

331 April 1971 (right) Based on the
330, the 'Light Show' model was
very much a guitar of its time. The
initial gimmicky idea was created
by an outside two-man design
team who then licensed it to
Rickenbacker, with production
commencing in 1970. The body
of the instrument contained a
number of lamps with colored
filters, and their constantly
changing pattern was visible through
the guitar's transparent top, providing
a light-show effect.

331 October 1971 (above) The
second version evolved from the earlier
'Type 1' (example from April 1971,
right) via a series of up-grades in
construction and components. The
revised design employed colored lights
instead of filters, an improved control
system using printed circuitry, and a
heavier-duty transformer for the
independent power supply.

1000 $129.50 (last seven in black, natural or fireglo finish); 600 (blond or turquoise blue) $179.50; 615 (fireglo) $329.50; 800 (turquoise blue) $215; 850 (turquoise blue or natural) $225. *310-375 Series, Thin Hollow Bodies* (fireglo or natural): 310 $294.50; 315 $344.50; 320 $309.50 ; 325 $359.50; 330 $319.50; 335 $369.50; 340 $339.50; 345 $384.50; 360 $394.50; 365 $439.50; 370 $409.50; 375 $459.50. *F Series, Thin Full Hollow Bodies* (fireglo or natural): 330F $344.50; 335F $399.50; 340F $359.50; 345F $399.50; 360F $419.50; 365F $474.50; 370F $439.50; 375F $489.50. *Thick Body Series* (autumnglo or natural): 381 $498.

IF SIX WAS TWELVE

During 1963 it was decided at Rickenbacker that the company would develop an electric 12-string guitar. Acoustic 12-strings had been around for some time, not least in the 1930s when blues artists like Leadbelly and Blind Willie McTell popularized their big, clanging sound. The folk boom in the early 1960s gave an even bigger lift to the acoustic 12-string's appeal, but electric 12-strings were far less common. One of the first must have been that made around 1955 by Stratosphere of Springfield, Missouri. It was tuned differently from the 12-string standard, which was later established on an electric 12-string by Danelectro's early Bellzouki model, launched by the New York-based company around 1961.

F.C. Hall thought a Rickenbacker electric 12-string would be a good idea, and asked Dick Burke to come up with a way of incorporating the necessary 12 tuners into a headstock of Rickenbacker's normal size. Other 12-string guitars tended to range six tuners along each side of a necessarily elongated headstock, but Hall thought this looked ungainly.

Burke, who was head of Rickenbacker's woodshop at the time, began to consider the options. "I drilled around," he remembers, "and we worked it different ways." The scheme he came up with was brilliantly simple, an imaginative leap that solved the problem Hall had posed, and in the process created an attractive piece of design.

Burke kept the existing six tuners where they normally were, three on each side of the headstock. He then routed two parallel channels into the face of the headstock – like the slots on a classical guitar, but not going all the way through. Burke attached the second set of six tuners at 90 degrees to the first set, the keys facing 'backwards' – again, like a classical guitar, with strings attached into the tuners' spindles in the channels – and gently altered the overall outline. "That headstock didn't take very long to come up with," he says. "We thought about putting the rout all the way through, in fact I think I made a couple like that, but it looked better without. We ended up with a rout just a little way in."

On a 12-string guitar the normal six strings are doubled up. With the tuning system that Rickenbacker and most contemporary 12-string makers used, the lower four pairs each consisted of a normally-tuned string plus a string an octave higher, while each of the top two pairs are tuned in unison. This strengthening of the guitar's sound through octave and unison doubling produces the classic 12-string 'jangling' sound, almost as if two guitars were playing together.

Rickenbacker made at least three experimental 12-string guitars in 1963. The very first, a 360-style instrument, was fitted with a gold pickguard and 'oven' knobs, and had the higher string of the octave pairs nearest the player, which was the system later adopted by most other makers of electric 12-strings. The later two Rickenbacker 12-strings made in 1963 were a 620-style guitar and another 360, both fitted with the white pickguard and black knobs that the company were beginning to introduce at the time. These two guitars also adopted what became Rickenbacker's own standard method of placing the normal string of each pairing above the octave string. With this idiosyncratic arrangement, the player's downstroke will hit a bass string before an octave string, giving a slightly different sound.

The first 12-string went to showband singer, fiddle-player and guitarist Suzi Arden, whose Suzi Arden Show was a regular at the Golden Nugget in Las Vegas. She had visited the Rickenbacker offices in November 1963, and the company had provided the country-oriented band with Rickenbacker amplifiers. Arden's three backup guitarists also received Rickenbacker guitars and a bass. "Mr Hall brought me the 12-string," Arden remembers. "It was the first one, his 'model.' He always brought me new things he was doing. He said: Try this new 12-string out, see how you like it. I did, and I wouldn't let him take it back," she laughs.

"I was playing a Martin electric six-string at the time," Arden continues, "but the Rickenbacker was so sweet, sounded so good, and it added to my show so much. It made a sharp, beautiful sound, there's nothing I think sounds as beautiful as a Rickenbacker 12. I could play all the chords on it real easy, and being electric also I loved it. I used the 12-string always from that point on, for the next 20-something years."

Having made the three 12-string samples, and with one in active use, Rickenbacker must have been sure by the end of 1963 that such an instrument would make a viable addition to the line for 1964. Meanwhile Rickenbacker amused itself by producing a neat little build-it-yourself solidbody electric guitar kit aimed at the Christmas 1963 gift market. The Astro Kit guitar, designed by Marvin Boyd, came as a box of 25 parts, including unpainted body and neck. "It will be educational," claimed the instructions, "and lots of fun to assemble." They also suggested that "if you are not familiar with wood finishes you contact your favorite paint store for helpful hints." It's not difficult to picture the cozy Christmas scene as a paint-streaked Astro Kit recipient finally proceeded to Step 13 in the instructions: "Stick plate to top side of head."

A CHARMING FELLOW

During 1963, the British distribution company Rose-Morris again contacted F.C. Hall about handling Rickenbacker guitars in the U.K. Hall also received similar enquiries from two other British operations: Jennings, who already distributed Fender in the U.K.; and Gibson's agent in Britain, Selmer. Now well aware of the growing popularity of The Beatles, Roy Morris of Rose-Morris included a magazine picture of the group with the letter he sent to Rickenbacker in November. "This shows the Rickenbackers used by the group I mentioned to you," he wrote to Hall. The following month, Morris and his colleague Maurice Woolf visited Hall in Santa Ana and clinched the UK distribution deal, with an initial order of 450 pieces comprising solid model 615, hollow models 325, 335 and 345, and a bass.

Maurice Woolf of Rose-Morris mentioned in a letter to F.C. Hall in December, "We think it would be an excellent idea if

you, as the manufacturer of Rickenbacker Guitars, were to contact the Beatles' manager and offer them a certain amount of American publicity on their forthcoming visit to the States." He then gave Brian Epstein's Liverpool address, explaining that Epstein was The Beatles' manager "and is, I believe, a very charming fellow. It is impossible to exaggerate [The Beatles'] influence at the present moment in this country. We will be getting in touch with him eventually but an initial letter from you could be very important for us all."

MEET THE BEATLES

Hall remembers that he had heard about The Beatles through one of his salesmen, possibly Harold Buckner. "He told me that on one of their recordings they used a Rickenbacker guitar, you could tell from the sound. When I heard they were coming to the United States, I called Epstein and made a date to meet with them in New York." Hall phoned Epstein early in January 1964 and arranged a meeting for the following month, a few days after the group would set foot in the U.S. for the first time. Hall wrote to confirm the meeting, telling Epstein he would have amps, echo units "and some other new products by Rickenbacker available for the boys to try out while they are here in New York." Perhaps the mention of "new products" indicates that Hall had already thought that the brand new 12-string might be good to include in the selection he intended to show The Beatles during the upcoming meeting.

Hall was used to encouraging well-known players to use Rickenbacker merchandise, and had arranged deals in the 1950s with stars such as Rick Nelson and Jim Reeves. But he was becoming aware that additional use of Rickenbacker products by The Beatles would assume far greater importance. "I have a definite date to talk to the Beatles in New York," he wrote to salesman Harold Buckner in late January. "However *please* do not mention this to a soul as I do not want our competition to know I will be there in New York while they are there." Hall added a P.S.: "The Beatles now have the number one single record in the United States and the number three best selling album."

Rickenbacker set up a special display at the Savoy Hilton hotel in New York, and on February 8th The Beatles – whose

37

381JK 1989 (right) This signature model, introduced in 1988, was based on the carved-body 381 favored by Steppenwolf's John Kay during the early 1970s. Built to his specifications, the new guitar incorporated various updated features, such as humbucking pickups, active circuitry, phase switching and coil-tapping facilities.

John Kay (right) The Steppenwolf guitarist is pictured holding his signature model, made as a limited edition of 250. The jetglo finish is complemented by a silver plastic, two-tier pickguard.

381/12V69 1993 (left) In 1989 Rickenbacker 'reissued' a model that had not been a production instrument – only a small number of 12-string 381s were made in the late 1960s.

381 1969 (right) Rickenbacker reintroduced the 381 into their catalog in the late 1960s. The new version came with a modified white plastic, two-tier pickguard.

381 1969 side view (above) As can be seen here, the body front and back of this model have a pronounced 'German carve', a characteristic styling idea of leading Rickenbacker designer Roger Rossmeisl.

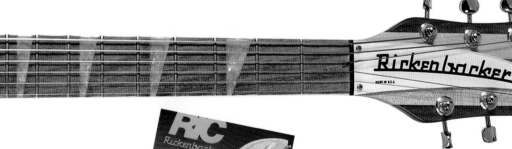

Hand-Crafted Quality 1989 (right) This explained Rickenbacker's manufacturing techniques. An earlier edition used a shot of an oriental worker at the factory, replaced by this picture of Adolph Rickenbacker, emphasizing the company's long American history.

381 1969 (above) The Thick-body models were originally introduced under the Capri heading in 1958. They used the 'sweeping crescent' shape, but impressively carved body fronts and backs added significant individual character. Early examples had differing features, and production was limited, the 381 being the most numerous. Manufacture ceased in the early 1960s, starting again at the close of the decade. The 381 was then equipped with this five control layout and two-tier white pickguard.

arrival in the States to play the Ed Sullivan TV show and three concerts had caused unrivaled scenes of fan mania – were due to come over and take a look at the guitars and equipment. Unfortunately, George Harrison was unwell and stayed in bed at the Plaza Hotel. But Rickenbackers were not entirely new to Harrison. Of course he was familiar with Lennon's, but very briefly in summer 1963 Harrison had used a Rickenbacker model 425, apparently bought when he and his brother visited their sister in the U.S. However, Harrison soon returned to his more accustomed Gretsch Country Gentleman guitar.

WITH THE BEATLES

F.C. Hall remembers the arrival of the three fit Beatles at the Rickenbacker display in New York. "They came over to our suite, and we showed them the new 12-string we'd just developed [the company's second 360/12]. John Lennon wanted to know if he could take it back and show it to George Harrison. He asked me if I would go with them back to their suite, so we carried it across the park there in New York."

Harrison evidently enjoyed the new 12-string. "Straight away I liked that you knew exactly which string was which," he recalled in a BBC interview. "Some 12-strings... you're turning the wrong [tuner] there's so many of them."

Hall again: "George was playing it and the telephone rang and John Lennon went to answer it in another room. He came back pretty soon and he said some radio station, I forget which, wanted to talk to George Harrison because they'd heard he was ill. Pretty soon I heard George telling them about the instrument that John Lennon had brought over for him to look at, over the air. They said do you like that instrument? And George said: I sure do! They said well if we buy it for you, will you play it? And he said *yes*," Hall laughs.

In fact there is some confusion as to whether the radio station bought that original 12-string for Harrison, or a later guitar. Rickenbacker today insists that it alone presented the original 12-string to Harrison.

Rickenbacker certainly gave a guitar to Lennon: a black 325 model with the new five-control layout, presumably intended to replace his somewhat road-weary early-style 325. F.C. Hall also promised to send Lennon a special one-off 12-string

version of the 325, and Beatles manager Brian Epstein requested a second 360-style 12-string for another of his now famous charges, Gerry Marsden of Gerry & The Pacemakers.

For the two Ed Sullivan Show appearances in New York on February 9th (one went out live, the other was taped for later broadcast) Lennon used his old 325, but for The Beatles' second live Sullivan appearance, broadcast seven days later from the Deauville Hotel in Miami, Florida, Lennon gave his new five-knob 325 its public debut. The two live shows were outrageously popular, each receiving an unprecedented American TV audience of some 70 million viewers. No doubt F.C. Hall allowed himself a smile as he watched the group perform in the New York TV studio.

After their thoroughly successful invasion of the United States The Beatles returned to EMI's Abbey Road studio in north London to record their next single, 'Can't Buy Me Love.' It was Harrison's 21st birthday, and he celebrated by giving his new Rickenbacker 12-string its first recorded outing on the B-side, 'You Can't Do That,' while Lennon also used his new 325. In the wake of this recording debut, an April issue of *Melody Maker*, the top British pop newspaper at the time, called the 12-string "the beat boys' secret weapon – it could become *the* musical instrument of 1964."

That Beatles single was released in mid-March, and in the U.S. it sold more than two million copies *in a week*. Both the tracks appeared on the soundtrack album for *A Hard Day's Night*, The Beatles' first feature film which was released in July. Harrison's 12-string makes an impressive film debut, both sonically and visually, and perhaps its most famous use on record is for the striking opening chord of the title song, 'A Hard Day's Night,' ringing out in typically jangling fashion. "That sound," Harrison recalled, "you just associate with those early 1960s Beatle records. The Rickenbacker 12-string sound is a sound on its own."

Harrison and Lennon also began to use their new Rickenbackers on stage. In the summer of 1964 the group returned to the U.S. for more concerts, playing the Hollywood Bowl in Los Angeles on August 23rd, where F.C. Hall and his son John were in the audience. They must have been delighted to see George Harrison and John Lennon step on stage carrying the 12-string and the 325 and use them to launch into the opening song, 'Twist & Shout.' Lennon had also by now received his one-off 325-style 12-string, but does not appear to have used it to any great effect. The tuning and playability problems associated with 12 strings on a slim, short-scale neck do not make this surprising.

EXPORTS AND F-HOLES

Roy Morris of Rose-Morris had written to F.C. Hall in late 1963 concerning the Rickenbacker guitars that the British company were about to start selling in the UK. "I understand that models 325, 335 and 345 will all be manufactured with the same 'traditional' f-holes which we saw on the 325 you had in your showroom, and that all instruments will be manufactured in your 'fireglo' finish," Morris wrote, concluding: "We may eventually find it more convenient to allocate our own stock numbers, in which case [these] should appear [on the packing carton]."

From the early 1960s Rickenbacker had made some of the short-scale 300 series semi-acoustic guitars with an f-hole, others with a 'solid' top. Morris and Woolf evidently took a liking to the more traditional soundhole, and asked for it also to be used instead of Rickenbacker's standard scimitar-shaped soundhole on the bigger semi-acoustic guitars. So it was that most of the semi-acoustics that Rickenbacker subsequently made for export had f-holes. These export guitars (to Canada, Australia and other places as well as to the U.K.) also used Rickenbacker's earlier style of plain black control knobs.

However, Rickenbackers with f-holes were also sold in the U.S., referred to by Rickenbacker with an 'S' for 'Special' suffix (for example, 345S). As Dick Burke recalls: "It was the same instrument except for the f-hole – using the same jig. It was a simple job to change to the f-hole in production, it just meant changing a few screws on the jig and putting in a new pattern."

Rose-Morris received their initial deliveries of Rickenbackers in the first half of 1964 and did adopt their own stock numbers, as Roy Morris had predicted. At that time Rose-Morris imported all manner of guitars and other musical equipment, resulting in a large catalog that used four-figure numbers as stock references. Their model 1846, for example,

was an Eko hollow-body electric from Italy, model 1970 a Top Twenty solidbody electric from Japan, and model 1998 a Rickenbacker 345S semi-acoustic electric from Santa Ana.

These were purely internal reference numbers that certainly did not appear on the guitars themselves, and had nothing to do with Rickenbacker. Rose-Morris catalogued their first Rickenbacker models, all non-deluxe vibrato-equipped models, as follows: 1998 (a 345S) priced £178/10/- (pounds/shillings/pence); 1997 (335S) £166/19/-; 1996 (325S) £166/19/-; and 1995 (615S) £141/15/-.

Roy Morris wrote to F.C. Hall in March 1964: "I have now been informed that the instruments which you provided during The Beatles' recent visit to the States were a model 325 for John Lennon and, to my considerable surprise, a 12-string instrument for George Harrison. I was not even aware that you made such an instrument, and obviously it will be necessary for me to have full details immediately; there can be little doubt that we will receive some demand for this instrument." This resulted in Rose-Morris adding later in 1964 a 12-string to their imported line of Rickenbackers. It had a bound body like Harrison's, but differed in its dot position markers on the fingerboard and traditional f-hole. Rose-Morris catalogued this as their model 1993, priced at £222/10/-.

HERE WE GO ROUND

Rickenbacker had added three electric 12-string models to the line during 1964: the 360/12, which was a 12-string 360 (i.e. two pickups, double-bound body, 'slash' soundhole and triangle fingerboard markers), first appearing on the July 1964 pricelist at $550; the 370/12 (effectively a three-pickup version of the 360/12), first appearing in 1964, although as it did not appear on a pricelist at that time it was probably a special order item; and the 450/12 which was a 12-string 450 (i.e. solidbody with two pickups), first appearing on the August 1965 pricelist at $294.50.

Around this time Rickenbacker introduced another body style for their 'deluxe' models 360, 360/12, 365, 370, 370/12 and 375. The new design had a streamlined, less angular look to the front of the body, with binding on the 'slash' soundhole and now only on the back edge of the body (see examples on

360F 1959 (above & left) The Thin Full-Body models appeared on Rickenbacker pricelists in early 1959, although prototypes had been displayed the previous year. The guitars were large in outline, but shallow in depth, hence the company's description.

375F 1964 (left) These guitars were the most conventional Rickenbackers in terms of shape, again originally listed under the Capri name until this title was dropped in 1960. The overall appearance has a Germanic feel, suggesting Roger Rossmeisl's design involvement once more. There were eight versions in the series, the model numbers adhering to standard company practice, but with an 'F' suffix denoting the body style. The 375F was top of the line, being a deluxe version with three pickups and vibrato tailpiece.

360F 1968 (left) Late 1960s examples departed from Rickenbacker's normal method of mounting controls on to the pickguard. They were now relocated on to the front of the body.

'Big R' brochure c1959 (above) Although only four pages thin, this was Rickenbacker's first literature to appear in color. It showed a representative selection of the range plus various design aspects.

360F/12 1968 (right) This was a late addition to the series, as only a few were made during the late 1960s. By 1973 it had become an official production item, offering the Deluxe 12-string spec in a conventional shape.

MODELS 360F-370F

The Deluxe Semi-acoustic Full Body Series brings new highlights to a guitar design, accepted for hundreds of years. The mellow sound of a true acoustic can be contrasted with solid treble sounds, all within one instrument. Shaped to appeal to the traditional guitarist, this series incorporates features appealing to all guitarists. Both sides of the Maple body and the Walnut-laminated Maple neck are hand bound with handsome white binding. Mother of Pearl fret inlays adorn the Brazilian Rosewood fingerboard. All metal parts are heavily chromed for maximum wear and beauty. Rickenbacker custom circuitry gives this instrument precise, controllable sound. Five variable controls match the instrument to any amplifier, and a convenient switch allows instantaneous tone change. This instrument is available in natural grain Fireglo and Mapleglo. Solid color Azureglo, Jetglo, and Burgundyglo. The optional Rickenbacker Ac'cent vibrato provides a nuance of true-pitch variation. Rich-O-Sound output is standard on this series, allowing a true stereo sound.

Sunflowers in '68 (above) The 1968 catalog came with op-art black and white cover, but the guitars were photographed in glorious color, the 360F and 370F posing in a field of sunflowers.

pages 46/47). It was designed to be more comfortable for the player, and while the new streamlined design was from 1964 the main production style used for the models mentioned, old style versions (i.e. with body bound front and back, with 'sharp' edges) remained available on special order.

Rickenbacker's press release described the new design as having "rounded edges" and "contoured shaping", continuing: "The smooth roundness avoids all that is harsh and yields flowing lines for smooth, easy playing – and handling." The new style did not entail much change at the factory, and in fact was only a cosmetic alteration: the old-style 'sharp edge' and the new-style 'round edge' could be produced from the same body blank. "Everything was the same," reports Dick Burke, who is still involved in producing new style and old style bodies at Rickenbacker today. "For the rounded style we just shape the top of it, instead of putting in the binding groove and adding the binding."

Another change that Rickenbacker made in the early 1960s was to the tailpiece, which previously had been a rather plain 'trapeze'-shaped piece of flat metal. During 1963 Rickenbacker introduced a striking new tailpiece in the shape of a large 'R.' Dick Burke explains its origins: "We copied that from the Washington Redskins football team – they had a similar 'R' for Redskins on their hat. Mr Hall wanted a new tailpiece, and obviously 'R' went with Rickenbacker. I remembered seeing those Redskins' hats and that the way the tail of the 'R' came up looked good, so we just copied it from there," he laughs.

JUST GET AN ELECTRIC GUITAR

The Beatles film *A Hard Day's Night* had a profound effect on young people in 1964, inspiring many to get an electric guitar and form a pop group. It looked like so much fun. And with Rickenbackers so prominent in the film, the company benefited enormously. John Hall says, "The Beatles gave the company a kind of visibility and unpaid-for advertising that we couldn't possibly have garnered any other way."

Rickenbacker added a large third building to the factory in Santa Ana to cope with the new demand, and as F.C. Hall recalls in wonderfully understated fashion: "There were musicians who wanted to make the same sound as The Beatles

had, so they started purchasing Rickenbackers too." One such musician was a Californian named Jim (later Roger) McGuinn, whose group The Jet Set were about to change their name to The Byrds.

McGuinn was playing a Gibson acoustic 12-string to which he'd added a pickup, trying to get a sound like that of his main influence, The Beatles. "One night we all went down to the Pix theater in Hollywood to see *A Hard Day's Night*," McGuinn recalls. "We carefully noted the brands and models of their instruments. John had a little black 325 Rickenbacker, Paul had a Hïfner bass, Ringo played Ludwig drums, and George had a Gretsch six-string and a Rickenbacker that looked like a six-string until he turned sideways. The camera revealed another six strings hidden in the back. I knew right then the secret of their wonderful guitar sound. It was a Rickenbacker 12-string!

"The Byrds had gotten a $5000 loan to buy new instruments. The next day we went down to the local music shop and bought a Rickenbacker rounded-front mapleglo [natural finish] 360/12, along with a Gretsch six-string and a set of Ludwig drums. The new instruments gave us a sense of confidence that we hadn't had up to that point. We soon got a record deal on Columbia, and the Rickenbacker 12-string with the aid of electronic compression in the studio gave us the distinctive 'jingle jangle' sound that we would later be known for," he says.

McGuinn used his 360/12 to devastating effect on The Byrds' very first single, 'Mr Tambourine Man,' recorded at Columbia studios in Hollywood in January 1965 (released in June). Bob Dylan's lyrics even included that most perfect description of the Rickenbacker 12-string sound: "jingle jangle."

McGuinn fitted a Vox treble booster inside his original 360/12 for extra tonal emphasis. "That guitar was unfortunately stolen while we were performing at a college in New York," he remembers, "and I think I borrowed a fireglo 360 12-string [with 'old-style' body] until I could replace the first one with another rounded mapleglo 360/12 in 1966. I also added a Vox treble booster to that one, and it became my main guitar. It too was stolen, in late 1966." It must have been with

44

one of these guitars that McGuinn made another of The Byrds' most notable records, 'Eight Miles High,' recorded in January 1966, highlighted by its jagged, impressionistic 12-string solo.

In 1967 McGuinn and Byrds' vocalist/guitarist David Crosby went to the Rickenbacker factory and bought some custom guitars. McGuinn obtained a black 325, and a 370/12 with custom wiring (a volume control for each of the three pickups plus a master volume control, a selector to engage each pickup individually, and a tone-option selector). "I used the 370/12 until the end of The Byrds in 1973," reports McGuinn, "but the three-quarter-neck 325 was too short for me to tune properly, and I gave it to my kids as a toy guitar."

As Fast as We can Make Them

Production was continuing to grow at Rickenbacker in the late 1960s as demand for their guitars increased. A note from F.C. Hall to a customer in September 1966 typifies the position: "The delivery of Rickenbacker merchandise is falling further behind each month," he wrote. "At this time I cannot quote an exact delivery date for the orders you now have on file. Nevertheless we will do our best to see that your orders are filled as soon as possible."

Six months was not an unusual time for customers to wait in the late 1960s for delivery of their order of Rickenbacker guitars. Dick Burke estimates the busiest period as 1965-1968, and he recalls a peak of 103 workers at the Rickenbacker factory at the time. The name of the sales/distribution company was changed in 1965 from the old Radio & Television Equipment Co. to the more appropriate Rickenbacker Inc., and the sales office was moved in 1966 from South Main to East Stevens in Santa Ana. The name of the manufacturing company remained Electro String.

One consequence of all this success was that Rickenbacker was willing to indulge inventors who came to the company with new ideas for guitars. Through the second half of the 1960s and into the early 1970s the company came up with a series of relatively bizarre variations on instruments which most other makers probably would not have allowed to go beyond the drawing-board stage. We'll consider some of these now.

The 'Sceusa neck' was a special asymmetrical neck profile

available on a few instruments. It echoed earlier attempts by makers such as Epiphone and Burns to provide a shape better suited to the natural 'arch' of the player's hand by exaggerating the curve of the back of the neck toward the bass side. But it felt strange, and like the others the Sceusa neck was not popular. It was soon dropped from Rickenbacker's options. The company's one-year agreement with Peter Sceusa expired in April 1964.

Rickenbacker's 'string converter' guitars first appeared in 1966. Inventor James E. Gross came up with a converter 'comb' mounted to the body of a 12-string that could be manipulated to remove from play all or some of the second strings of each pair (see pictures on pages 23 and 34). Gross wrote in his explanatory letter to Rickenbacker of the converter's ability to allow single strings to be used for bass notes while retaining unison pairs for the higher strings "for a dirty 'twang' or mandolinish sound". He also said that the converter made the 12-string easier to tune "by starting with the six and then tuning the secondary six to the first six", and that it could facilitate a quick change from 12-string to six-string (and back) at the flip of a switch. "It would add little cost to production," Gross concluded, "yet would attract a great deal of plus business to the company and the 12-string guitar."

Rickenbacker went ahead with the converter — "Now two guitars in one!" said the publicity — and in the July 1966 pricelist showed three models with the chrome converter 'comb' fitted to the body: the 336/12 (in other words a convertible 330/12) at $529.50; the 366/12 (360/12) at $579.50; and the 456/12 (450/12) at $339.50. In each case these were priced between $45 and $55 more than the non-convertible versions.

Skewed Frets, Colored Lights

Another oddity was Quilla H ('Porky') Freeman's design for a guitar body with 'invisible' pickups, actually situated under the pickguard. Freeman had previously teamed up with Fender, who built prototypes and even put proposed Marauder guitars in the official 1965/66 catalog, but they never went into production.

Rickenbacker made an agreement with Freeman in 1967,

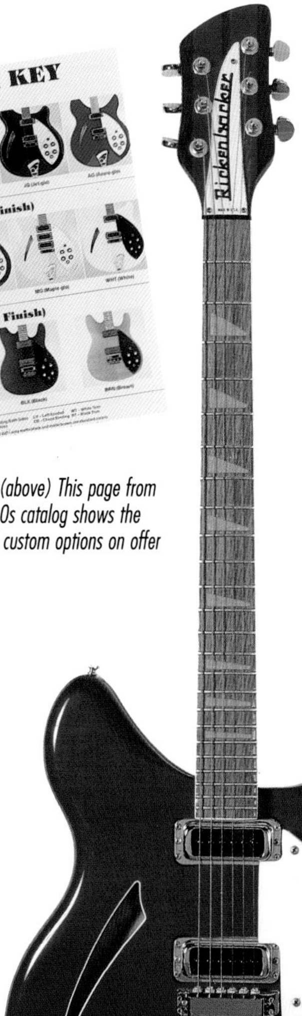

360 1975 (left) Top of the Thin Hollow Body series launched in 1958 were the 360-375 models, with appropriate deluxe features of bound body and neck, plus triangle position markers. In 1964 Rickenbacker revised the overall appearance of these up-market versions by simply rounding the front edge of the body, making the guitars look significantly different. The sweeping crescent profile was still apparent, but now with blunt rather than sharp pointed horns on both cutaways, and the lack of front binding softened the outline still further.

COLOR KEY
STANDARD

CUSTOM (Glossy Finish)

CUSTOM (Matte Finish)

Color Key (above) This page from an early 1980s catalog shows the standard and custom options on offer at that time.

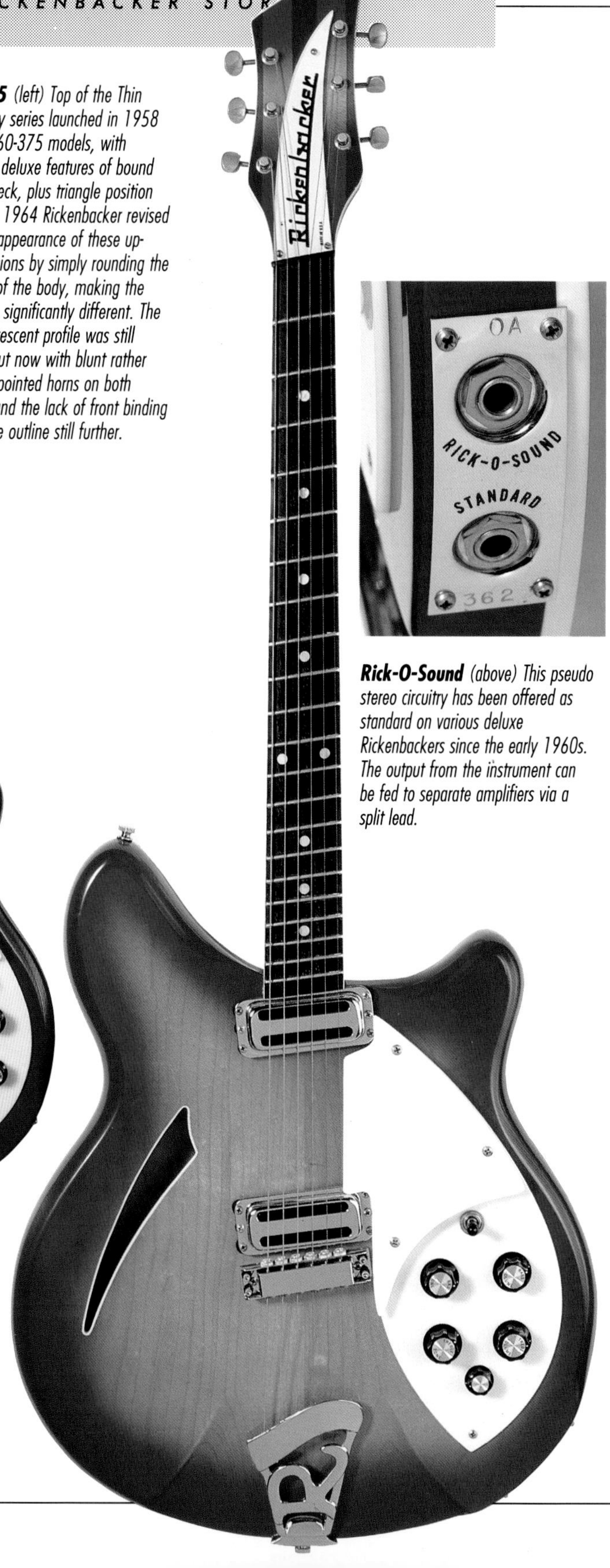

OA

RICK-O-SOUND

STANDARD

362

Rick-O-Sound (above) This pseudo stereo circuitry has been offered as standard on various deluxe Rickenbackers since the early 1960s. The output from the instrument can be fed to separate amplifiers via a split lead.

360SF 1968 (right) In 1968 an unusual feature was introduced – slanted frets. These matched 'natural finger angle', supposedly providing easier and faster playing. With the nut, pickups and bridge also sloping, such guitars looked odd and were never popular. The example shown is unusual, being a 360 but lacking the normal deluxe triangle position markers.

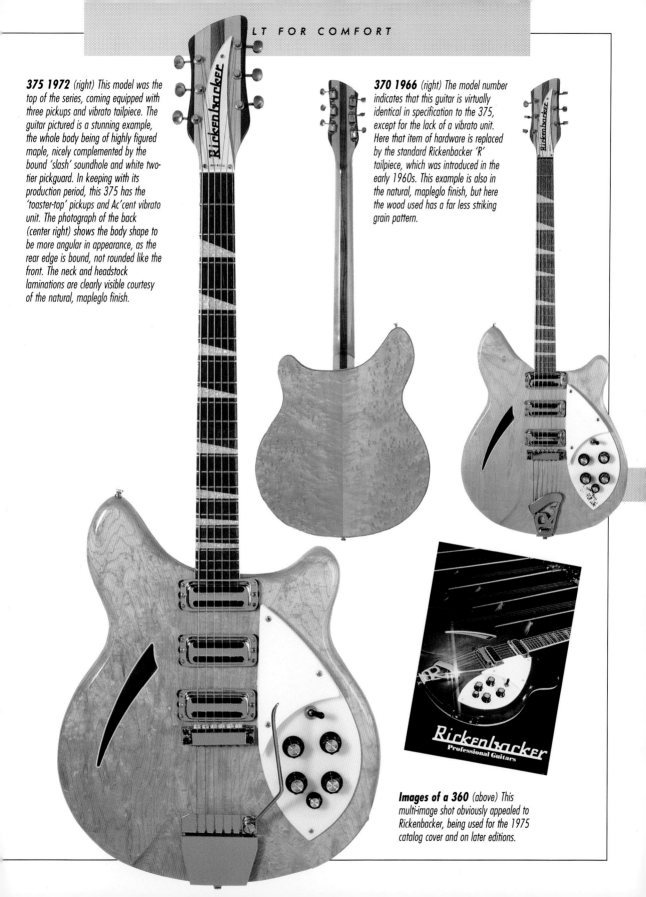

375 1972 (right) This model was the top of the series, coming equipped with three pickups and vibrato tailpiece. The guitar pictured is a stunning example, the whole body being of highly figured maple, nicely complemented by the bound 'slash' soundhole and white two-tier pickguard. In keeping with its production period, this 375 has the 'toaster-top' pickups and Ac'cent vibrato unit. The photograph of the back (center right) shows the body shape to be more angular in appearance, as the rear edge is bound, not rounded like the front. The neck and headstock laminations are clearly visible courtesy of the natural, mapleglo finish.

370 1966 (right) The model number indicates that this guitar is virtually identical in specification to the 375, except for the lack of a vibrato unit. Here that item of hardware is replaced by the standard Rickenbacker 'R' tailpiece, which was introduced in the early 1960s. This example is also in the natural, mapleglo finish, but here the wood used has a far less striking grain pattern.

Images of a 360 (above) This multi-image shot obviously appealed to Rickenbacker, being used for the 1975 catalog cover and on later editions.

but again the idea did not reach the marketplace. Nonetheless the company made at least one prototype, an unusual guitar built in April 1968 that did not duplicate any of Rickenbacker's normal body shapes. It had *two* 'slash' soundholes in a single cutaway bound body finished in fireglo, and a large semi-transparent pickguard under which the four buried pickups could just be seen.

'Slant fret' Rickenbackers first appeared in trial runs at the factory around 1968. The idea was brought to the company by one Henry C. Perez, and an agreement was officially completed in 1971. Perez's original sketch dictates an eight-degree slant to frets, pickups, nut and bridge, with the intention of making the guitar more comfortable to play. Rickenbacker's publicity said: "This slight slant of the frets across the fingerboard eliminates long chord reaches, reduces stretch length, and matches precisely the natural angle of the fretting fingers." The 1971 pricelist is the first to show the option, available on "most models" for an extra $100, and although rarely ordered after the early 1970s it was still noted on pricelists up to 1983. The slant fret feature was offered as standard on the 481 solidbody, introduced in 1974. Standard colours now were fireglo, azureglo (blue), jetglo (black) and burgundyglo (wine red).

F.C. Hall's son John had started to work full-time for Rickenbacker in 1969, and he recalls the reaction to the slant fret guitars: "You pick up a guitar with slanted frets and play it, and it feels great, no question about it. But as soon as you tell someone it's a slanted fret guitar, they look at it, do a double take, oh wow, it is... and they can't play it any more," he laughs. "We'd sometimes ship slant fret 360s to people who ordered a 360, and then we'd never hear anything from them. I think our general feeling was, well, if no one cares... forget it."

Last of the decidedly weird Rickenbackers was the light-show guitar, first introduced in 1970, with a clear plastic top through which a psychedelic array of colored lights would shine, flashing in response to the frequencies of the notes being played. It came with a special unit that plugged between guitar and amplifier. "This was a three-channel color organ," explains John Hall. "The three light circuits were sensitive in different frequency ranges: if low frequency notes were hit, the lowest channel would trigger and whatever color lights were

screwed into that channel would blink. Mid and high frequencies lit the other channels. The whole combination of them, in a chord for instance, and they didn't light."

The light-show system was introduced to the company by Stephen F. Woodman and Marshall Arm, although Rickenbacker modified the original design by developing their own printed circuit boards, adding silver-foil lining inside the body to increase the projection of the bulbs. The instrument proved unpredictable, especially as a result of over-heating, and has since been likened to playing a toaster with pickups. Roger McGuinn had a special 12-string light-show guitar built with slant frets and three pickups, which he used for 'Eight Miles High' at the end of The Byrds' shows in the early 1970s. It was perhaps the most bizarre Rickenbacker ever made – a rare prize indeed, given the number of oddities that have been made at the factory in Santa Ana.

SMASHING RICKS

In Britain during the second half of the 1960s the number of famous pop guitarists using Rickenbackers was on the increase. Among those seen in such stylish company were The Moody Blues' Denny Laine, The Animals' Hilton Valentine and, most notably, The Who's Pete Townshend, who adopted various six- and 12-string 300-series models, primarily in the group's classic 1965-66 period.

Townshend has said that he used a 12-string Rickenbacker on 'I Can't Explain,' recorded in January 1965, "as a chord machine" – but he soon became known just as much for the smashing time he had with his hapless guitars. "I sometimes feel very bad about having smashed up instruments which were particularly good ones," Townshend recalled on BBC Radio 1 in the 1980s, "but generally I was working with production-line instruments." (Witness some of Townshend's production-line destruction on page 31.)

The Beatles received more Rickenbackers in 1965. George Harrison was presented with a new-style 'rounded' 360/12 at a press conference in August at the start of their third US tour. Harrison accordingly used the guitar at least once on stage, for 'If I Needed Someone' during the group's Japanese concerts the following summer. John Lennon had dropped and damaged his black 325 in 1965 and was given a fireglo 325S/1996 by Rose-Morris as a temporary replacement.

THIN FULL BODY

Rose-Morris found that demand in the UK for Rickenbackers gradually declined in 1965 and 1966, and considered dropping the 325S/1996 in 1966. In 1967 Rose-Morris had 100 guitars back-ordered with Rickenbacker, and the British company decided to concentrate its efforts on models 335S/1997 and 345S/1998. Rose-Morris also began to investigate the possibility of importing Rickenbacker copies from an Italian manufacturer. In 1968 there was hardly any contact between Rickenbacker and Rose-Morris, and by 1969 business between the two companies had ceased. Rose-Morris had started to import Rickenbacker copies under its own Shaftesbury brand, an act which could hardly have been designed to please the Americans.

In 1967 Rickenbacker made some changes to the Thin Full-Body series, which had been running steadily since 1959, at least as far as the pricelist compiler was concerned. The standard 330F/340F/335F/345F models were dropped, and the deluxe 360F/370F/365F/375F models redesigned with the controls laid out in a curving line near the edge of the body, no longer mounted on a pickguard (see page 43). Dick Burke remembers that F.C. Hall asked for such an arrangement, and that once again it fell to Burke to find a solution. He had to come up with a way of getting the controls mounted on the body, without gaining access to the semi-hollow body from the back. "So we made a special hole about two-and-a-half inches in diameter under the big pickguard," Burke recalls. "We would feed the controls into that hole and then, just like a surgeon, use a long tool to pull each one through the small individual holes on the body, locking them into position." The new style of F models was released during 1968.

Burke reckons that it was about this time that demand for Rickenbackers began to decline, and estimates that the slower years were 1969, 1970 and 1971. From a peak of just over 100 factory workers at one point during the busy 1965-1968 period, there was a time between 1969 and 1971 when just eight workers were employed at the factory, he recalls. The

company's valuable link with The Beatles was of course severed when the group split in 1970, little in the way of new Rickenbacker models was forthcoming to excite guitar players, and anyway, the fashionable instrument of the time was the Gibson Les Paul. Fortunately for Rickenbacker their bass guitars gained in popularity in the early 1970s after bassists such as Chris Squire of Yes were seen using them, and production began to pick up again at Santa Ana, concentrating on four-string models.

A few changes were made to the guitar models at this time. In 1969 a new type of high output pickup called the Hi-Gain unit was introduced, and the same year saw the introduction of 24 frets for 330/360-family guitars, which until then had 21 frets as standard. Production of both 21-fret and 24-fret models continued into the 1970s, but by the middle of the decade the 21-fret versions had all but disappeared.

Around 1970 the deluxe 'triangle' fingerboard inlay was made less wide, as Dick Burke remembers: "We changed it at that time from all the way across to mid-way. Especially on a 12-string, I think it makes for a stronger neck when the inlay doesn't go all the way across. On the older version we used to take more wood out, and that would weaken the neck." In the mid-1970s Rickenbacker stopped equipping guitars with the Ac'cent vibrato, and did not reinstate this unit until 1985.

TOOLING AND PLUG-INS

In the early 1970s Rickenbacker introduced what for them was a radically different design, their first new body shape for many years, and which unusually for the company was teamed with a bolt-on neck. The solidbody design finally appeared in public as the model 430, launched in 1971 as a lower-cost guitar ($249.50) reacting to cheaper imported guitars appearing on the market. The 430 was based on tooling developed for a proposed line of models devised by Forrest White, who worked briefly for Rickenbacker around 1970. White had been production chief at Fender from 1954 to 1967, and it is not therefore too surprising that styling of the 430 is closer to Fender than anything Rickenbacker had made previously. It did not prove a very successful seller, being neither classic Rickenbacker nor especially exciting.

49

'Older' Roger McGuinn (left)
Shown with the signature model
12-string produced by Rickenbacker
to his specifications.

'Younger' Roger McGuinn
(above) Roger McGuinn when he was
'younger than yesterday' in The Byrds,
playing a 1960s Rickenbacker.

370/12RM 1988 (above) Roger
McGuinn's signature model 12-string
was introduced in 1988, as a limited
edition of 1000. Unlike his 1960s

original it came with a 12-saddle
bridge, plus active tone and
compression circuitry governed by a
revised control set-up.

360/12SPC Tuxedo 1987
(below) The Tuxedo finish was a
custom cosmetic option offered during
the late 1980s. The complete
instrument came in polar white,

unusually including the fingerboard,
while all hardware and plastic parts
were black. The contrasting effect
was striking, as can be seen on
this example.

360/12 1980 (above) This more rounded body styling was introduced for deluxe 360-series instruments during 1964. It contrasts with the earlier angular style which was bound both front and back, and Rickenbacker continued to make both types. The guitar shown is a proposed variant that never went into production, designed to celebrate the company's 50th year in 1981. It was fitted with gold tuners, and carried an anniversary logo.

51

360/12 L/H 1970 (above) Left-handed versions of any production instrument are none too common, and Rickenbackers are no exception. This 'mirror image' 360 12-string looks more unusual than many, thanks to the overall size of the guitar, and the visual reversal of recognized Rickenbacker styling characteristics including the logo which slopes in the 'wrong' direction.

A year or so later John Hall, by now much more involved in the day to day running of the company, came up with a proposed guitar design called the System 490. A trial guitar was made, with the 430 body style, and the System 490 even appeared on 1973 and 1974 pricelists, but was never actually produced. The 490 was based on the idea of plug-in pickup and electronics modules, drawing from Hall's interest in computers and electronics. "At that time I was impressed with the whole idea of modularity and upgradeability," he recalls, "and didn't understand why that shouldn't be so in a guitar. There were complex molds involved to make the pickguards so they could pop in and out, designed such that the pickups automatically located into spring contacts in the pickguards. It was a mechanical design exercise, more than anything."

ADAPTING THE BASS LINE

Another new body shape appeared at this time, although it was really only new to Rickenbacker's six-string guitar lines. The 480, introduced in 1973, used the body styling made famous by the company's basses, which had first appeared in 1957. The most distinctive visual aspect was the elongated left horn, and the idea to produce a guitar version was probably F.C. Hall's. Dick Burke says that, given the great popularity of Rickenbacker's basses in the early 1970s, marketing sense must have dictated the creation of such a guitar model. "It would look good if the guys were playing both in a band," he says. "I guess Mr Hall felt that if you had a guitar that was similar it might sell the instrument along with the bass."

A year later the 481 was added, with slanted frets and twin humbucking pickups, providing another less than popular outing for Henry Perez's new angle on fretting, and in 1980 the three-pickup 483 was added to the 'bass body' family. These models stayed in the line until 1983.

A few custom double-neck guitars had been made for individual Rickenbacker customers in the 1960s, but in 1975 the company's first production double-necks appeared. There were two types: the 4080 was modeled on Rickenbacker's electric bass body style, while the 362 enlarged upon the familiar 360 body theme.

Double-neck electric guitars had been made since the mid-1950s by various companies, and the main aim was effectively to provide two guitars in one – usually a combination of six-string guitar and four-string bass, or six-string and 12-string guitars. Of course the resulting instruments were necessarily heavy, and players tended to limit their stage use of double-necks to a few appropriate songs.

Roger McGuinn had one of the earliest 362 double-necks, built for him before the official production run started, and he echoes the general feeling about such instruments: "I got mine in 1972. I found it a little too heavy to use for the whole show and would use my 370/12 for the most part." Rickenbacker's double-necks were expensive, and clearly premium instruments. As one might expect they were manufactured in very small batches. Since the beginning of the modern company's guitar production in 1954 right through to today, Rickenbacker's minimum run has been 25 instruments. For the double-necks, however, Dick Burke recalls that they would make as few as 10 or 15 at a time.

In March 1976 a sad occurrence was the death at the age of 89 of Adolph Rickenbacker – who of course had not been involved with the guitar company for over 20 years. In 1978 Rickenbacker Inc. moved offices, again within Santa Ana, from East Stevens to South Main, while the factory stayed at the same location on Kilson where it had been since the move from Los Angeles in 1962. The January 1978 pricelist listed 21 electric guitar models under three headings: *Electric Solid Body*: 420 $299; 430 $325; 450 $390; 450/12 $475; 460 $490; 480 $415; 481 $575; 620 $548; 900 $305; 950 $400; 4080 $1350; 4080/12 $1750. *Electric Thin Hollow Body*: 320 $565; 330 $550; 330/12 $725; 340 $570; 360 $650; 360/12 $770; 362/12 $1500; 370 $690. *Electric Thin Full Body*: 360/12F $638.

Following another peak in the mid 1970s, demand for Rickenbacker's instruments had begun to decline again, and Dick Burke recalls that by the early 1980s the workforce at Kilson was down to some 20 or 30 people.

BACK TO THE FUTURE

The market in so-called 'vintage' guitars had been building since the late-1960s. Some instruments were achieving high prices especially as a result of successful (and wealthy) guitarists of the day choosing to redistribute some of their earnings among eager vintage guitar dealers. Rickenbackers were by no means top of the list of vintage desirables, but nonetheless examples of the company's output from the 1950s and 1960s were beginning to fetch respectable sums.

In 1983 Rickenbacker made a half-hearted attempt to recreate some of their older models, trying to capture some of the vintage market, and produced the disappointingly inaccurate 'B' series models: the 360/12B ($1140), 320B ($1085) and 325B ($1185), as well as a bass. Another nod to their past occurred the same year with the 350 Liverpool ($820) and 355 Liverpool Plus ($920) models, essentially full-scale, 24-fret versions of the short-scale 325-style guitar associated with John Lennon – hence the 'Liverpool' tag.

A new generation of guitarists had started to take up Rickenbackers, and this helped the company's climb back to popularity during the 1980s. Among the most notable and visible players of Rickenbackers at the time were (in the U.S.) Peter Buck of REM, whose debut album appeared in 1983, and (in the U.K.) Johnny Marr of The Smiths, whose first LP was issued the following year. The jangling, rhythmic thrust of Rickenbackers was once more to be heard at the heart of some of pop's most vibrant offerings. "Some bands use keyboards to fill out a certain area of the sound," Marr said, "but I just automatically go for Rickenbacker 12-string."

Meanwhile Rickenbacker revived the body shape used for the 430 and the aborted System 490, launching in 1983 the 230 Hamburg and 250 El Dorado models – and suddenly Rickenbacker guitars had names! "That was something I really wanted to do. After all, every other company had names," laughs John Hall. "These instruments were feeling like bastards, with no names of their own. So we started thinking, and since then we've given names to the new instruments... as well as numbers, of course."

As with the 430, the idea for the Hamburg and El Dorado was to make a lower cost, simple looking guitar, and again Rickenbacker used the cheaper bolt-on-neck method of construction. John Hall collaborated with Rickenbacker's electronic engineer, George Cole, to come up with a clever electronic tweak. "They have passive boost circuits," Hall explains. "We sacrificed some of the power coming off the high-output pickups to drive the boost, instead of using a battery. The trouble was that the treble pickup didn't have all of that extra power. You could light up a flashlight bulb with the bass pickup, there was so much power. But the treble pickup was never quite as effective."

THE NEW VINTAGE

The business operation of Rickenbacker was changed fundamentally when John Hall officially took control in 1984, by which time F.C. Hall was 76 and ready to hand over the reins to his son. In fact John formed a new company, Rickenbacker International Corporation (RIC), which purchased the guitar-related parts of his father's Rickenbacker Inc. and Electro String companies.

With the new set-up in place, Hall started to change the sales organization of the company, established offices in England and Japan, and instituted a proper Rickenbacker vintage reissue program. The first results of this appeared that same year, in the shape of the 325V59, 325V63 and 360/12V64 models. "It was my goal to recreate very accurately those early guitars," he says. "I came up with that numbering system also, to allow for the fact that many of these guitars were the same model but were very different from year to year. For the 325 we had to do a V59 and a V63 – a Vintage 1959 and a Vintage 1963. Even though it was really the same guitar, a process of evolution had worked upon the instruments a little bit. So the number system was created to reflect that, and to allow us some flexibility to be able to reissue the same model of guitar but from different eras."

Hall says that a good deal of research was undertaken, looking at old photos, company records and original instruments, some of which Rickenbacker had in its own collection – a rarity among modern guitar companies. "Fortunately, in many cases we had the existing tooling, although in a lot of cases it was not marked. So it was a matter of finding an original guitar, holding it up to the patterns we have, and saying ah-hah, *that's* the one.

"I also sensed that we were more famous for what we had done than what we were doing – and at that particular time I'd

53

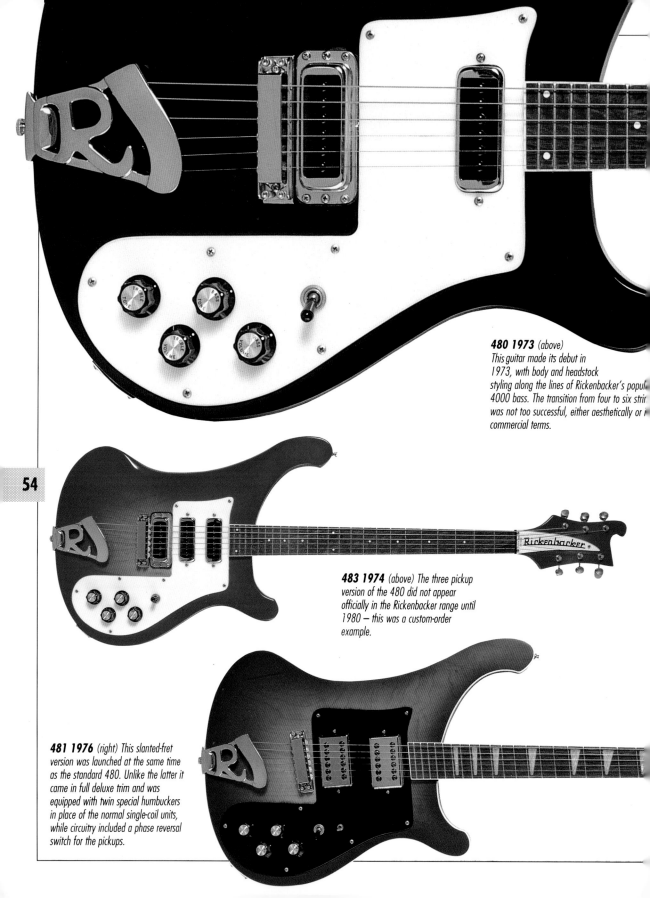

480 1973 (above)
This guitar made its debut in
1973, with body and headstock
styling along the lines of Rickenbacker's popul[ar]
4000 bass. The transition from four to six strin[gs]
was not too successful, either aesthetically or [in]
commercial terms.

483 1974 (above) The three pickup
version of the 480 did not appear
officially in the Rickenbacker range until
1980 – this was a custom-order
example.

481 1976 (right) This slanted-fret
version was launched at the same time
as the standard 480. Unlike the latter it
came in full deluxe trim and was
equipped with twin special humbuckers
in place of the normal single-coil units,
while circuitry included a phase reversal
switch for the pickups.

Glenn Frey (above) This former member of The Eagles joined the ranks of Rickenbacker's signature guitar endorsees in early 1992.

230 Glenn Frey 1993 (left) As the number designation suggests, this signature model is based on the standard 230 Hamburg design. However, features of this limited edition of 1000 include a more contoured body, hotter pickups and distinctive cosmetics.

250 El Dorado 1992 (left) The 250 El Dorado and the cheaper 230 Hamburg debuted in 1983, following on from the similarly shaped 430 which had been discontinued the previous year. The 250 came with appropriate high-end features such as bound body and fingerboard, and gold-plated metalwork.

55

200 Series catalog 1984 (right) This full colour edition introduced the new 230 Hamburg and 250 El Dorado models, extolling their attributes at great length. Some of the features described seem a little contradictory, such as the humbucking single-coil pickups and the battery-less active circuitry.

430 1976 (above) This solid appeared in 1971, and was about the nearest Rickenbacker have come to a Fender. This is not surprising, as the design originated from ex-Fender mainstay Forrest White during his tenure with Rickenbacker. The 430 was the culmination of various prototypes, and stayed in the line for 11 years.

say we were stagnant. But when I took over I had a lot more energy and wanted to take the thing a lot further, a lot faster, so it was fine for me to start tinkering with the formula. In that respect the vintage reissues made a lot of sense... and anyway, there were certainly many people asking us for guitars like that."

Dick Burke helped to redesign the company's truss-rod system at this time. "There are two single rods in the necks now, not two double-rods," he explains. "It's a much better system." A more visible change in 1985 resulted from Rickenbacker's revival of vibrato-equipped models after a break of some ten years. The company now manufactured the 'new' Ac'cent-style units in-house.

SIGNED, SEALED, DELIVERED

Another aspect of the company's history that Rickenbacker decided to exploit was their associations over the years with famous players. In the late 1980s Rickenbacker felt that they wanted to produce a guitar that offered something special, giving the potential customer the feeling that here was an instrument that only a small number of people would be privileged to own. In a sense, the idea was to echo the feelings that many players had about vintage guitars – but in a brand new model. In short, Rickenbacker's plan was to produce limited edition guitars.

But after many internal discussions, and informal talks with retailers and distributors, a more adventurous opportunity presented itself. Rickenbacker decided to make a range of 'signature' artist-endorsed guitars. In itself this was not a startlingly new marketing concept – the idea had been around for many years, at least since Gibson's Nick Lucas acoustic guitar of the late 1920s, and virtually all modern guitar companies have issued such 'signature' models. But it was new for Rickenbacker, and the company's added marketing twist was to combine this aspect with the attraction of a strictly limited production run.

Rickenbacker came up with the idea of issuing a numbered certificate with each of the limited edition guitars. This enabled a straightforward control to be exercised on the numbers produced, and emphasized to the customer that this was not

merely a mass-produced guitar, but an exclusive instrument.

At the time of writing, Rickenbacker has so far produced limited edition 'signature' guitars for seven artists. The Who's Pete Townshend was the first player to be so honored, in 1987, and he was followed by Roger McGuinn (ex-Byrds; edition released 1988), John Kay (ex-Steppenwolf; also 1988); Susanna Hoffs (The Bangles; 1988), John Lennon (1989); Tom Petty (1991); and Glenn Frey (ex-Eagles; 1992). There is also in existence a Jackson Browne prototype (pictured on page 62), although this design has yet to be finalized.

Townshend had used (and abused) some of Rickenbacker's f-hole export models in The Who's heyday during the mid-1960s. The company had already begun in 1987 to produce a non-vibrato reissue of the two-pickup '1997' (Rose-Morris numbering for a 335S), with export features such as the body f-hole and black control knobs. So it was logical to go one better for the Pete Townshend limited edition model, and Rickenbacker settled on a three-pickup '1998' (345S), but without the vibrato, which Townshend had never liked.

Contact was made with Townshend via Trevor Smith and Linda Garson at Rickenbacker's U.K. office. The artistic and historic value of such a project was stressed to Townshend, and the company explained that it wanted to make a limited run of the guitars. By its very nature this presented what to some musicians would be another bonus: such a deal would not necessarily entail a long-term association.

Townshend was still identified in many pop fans' minds with his habit in the 1960s of smashing up guitars – primarily Rickenbackers – on-stage. So it is likely that he was not alone in seeing the irony of a modern Rickenbacker Townshend model. "I'm quite surprised now that Rickenbacker are happy to have me sponsor an instrument which is so tied up with such an anarchic part of my career," he told BBC Radio 1 in 1987. "But it's the only guitar I've ever sponsored... and I've done it partly out of guilt."

Once all the details of the deal had been tidied up, there came the problem of just how limited to make this first Rickenbacker limited edition. John Hall recalls the calculations: "We thought we were *really* stepping off the deep end by allowing 250 of the 1998 Pete Townshend model to be produced – and they sold out in six weeks! Just like that. And of course," he laughs, "we then asked ourselves why on earth we hadn't gone with a thousand." Sales were indeed so rapid that the Townshend model was never featured in any of Rickenbacker's catalogs or pricelists of the period.

JINGLE JANGLE REVISITED

The next musician to be involved in Rickenbacker's special new program was Roger McGuinn, and a 'rounded' style 370/12 duly appeared in 1988, limited to a more substantial edition of 1000 guitars. McGuinn recalls: "When Rickenbacker's president John Hall called me to ask if I would be interested in participating in a limited edition signature series I was delighted. He asked what I wanted in my guitar. My first request was for an electronic compressor circuit to give my live performances the sound that we'd gotten on The Byrds' records," he says.

The circuit was primarily the work of Rickenbacker's engineer at the time, Bob Dessidaro, whom a colleague describes as being "very good at translating musicians' requirements into circuitry." John Hall says that it would have been useful to have had more time to spend on the circuit, "Especially in the area of conserving battery life and the nasty things that happen when the battery is dying. But in the end we ran out of time, because we had to introduce the guitar at the trade show," Hall explains.

The second item that McGuinn asked for on his signature guitar was a 12-saddle bridge, a unit conspicuous by its absence from any Rickenbacker 12-string before that time. An ordinary six-saddle bridge on any 12-string will be a source of tuning problems for guitarists who expect to play higher than the first few frets. So Rickenbacker relented, and for the first time in nearly 25 years installed a 12-saddle bridge on a 12-string guitar. To begin with, that was the only guitar on which it was available, but after the 370/12RM limited edition sold out during 1989 Rickenbacker began fitting it to some other of their 12-string models.

For the Pete Townshend model a logo of Townshend in classic arm-stretched 'windmilling' pose had been added to the pickguard. At first Rickenbacker looked for a similar identifying symbol for Roger McGuinn, and a logo of a pair of small 'granny' sunglasses, as worn by McGuinn at the time of The Byrds, was suggested. But a suitable image could not be found in time, and the guitar ended up with McGuinn's signature as the only adornment to the pickguard. As a nice personal touch, McGuinn signed all 1000 of the certificates that went out with his limited edition 370/12RM guitars.

McGuinn was clearly pleased with his signature guitar. "Rickenbacker's staff came up with an amazing circuit that sounded exactly like those early recordings. I loved it so much that I began using that circuit in the studio on my most recent work instead of the more costly studio compressors," he says. McGuinn was not alone in his praise for the instrument. Customers for the 370/12RM included George Harrison, Pete Townshend, Tom Petty, David Crosby, Peter Buck (REM) and Dave Stewart (ex-Eurythmics).

SMOKE AND LIGHTNING

John Kay, the ex-Steppenwolf guitarist, was the next choice for Rickenbacker's limited edition program. Kay had some ideas on what he wanted to incorporate into a guitar, especially a system of active electronics, and these details were worked out between Kay and Rickenbacker engineer Bob Dessidaro. Kay, who is color blind, specified the guitar's black and silver finish. His signature guitar had the highly carved body style of the 381-style models, but with more modern electronics and new pickups.

"The guitar is based on the model 381 which I first played in 1968 and used on various Steppenwolf records," Kay wrote in a company leaflet. He explained that the guitar incorporated humbucking pickups, active electronics and phase switching. Rickenbacker managed to fit the two coils of the quieter, thicker-sounding humbucking pickups into the same size casing as the traditional single-coil units. Kay concluded: "In these times of stamped out imitations, it is truly a pleasure to be associated with something genuine and of high quality." The 381JK was launched in 1988.

Discussions had started in 1987 with Susanna Hoffs of The Bangles about a signature Rickenbacker. Hoffs already played a 325, and said she'd like a 325-style body but with a full-scale

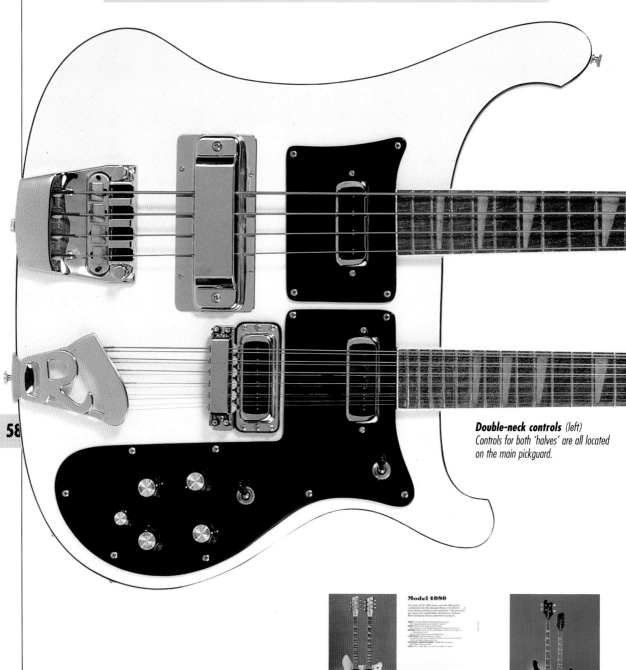

Double-neck controls (left)
Controls for both 'halves' are all located
on the main pickguard.

58

Catalog 1981 (right) This centerfold
spread from the full-color 1981 catalog
shows all three double-neck models
available at that time. Styling is based
on the standard single-neck instrument,

as indicated by the number
designation. On the left-hand page is
the 4080, not shown in this book. It
combined the 4001 bass with a
480-style guitar.

4080/12 1981 (below) This became a 'regular' production item in 1975, prior examples having been built on a custom-order basis only. It offered the 4001 bass and the 480 guitar in a somewhat unwieldy single package, with deluxe features as standard. Overall size is invariably a problem with double-neck designs, and the 4080 was no exception. In contrast to their large size, double-necks had little appeal, and manufacture ceased in 1985.

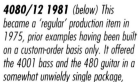

Angled necks (above/below) The necks are angled slightly away from one another to improve access.

Headstocks These are staggered due to differing scale lengths of the necks.

362/12 1975 (above) The model number indicates that this instrument was an amalgam of two 360s, the 12 and six-string versions. Aimed at the guitarist who spurned Rickenbacker's more compact 12/6 Convertible, this thin hollow-bodied beast offered an impressive if weighty alternative. As with the 4080, it was added to the line in 1975, and enjoyed a subsequent ten-year production span, even if few were actually built.

neck like the more recent 350 Liverpool, and all in white. Rickenbacker also had it in mind to make a guitar that incorporated some of the more contemporary features that musicians had been requesting from the company, such as a pickup layout of two single-coils and a humbucker.

Brian Carman (who worked for Rickenbacker from 1965-1974 and 1984-1993) and Dick Burke built the white Hoffs guitar by hand, completing it after several months' work. Derek Davis, vice president at Rickenbacker from 1986 to 1991, remembers taking the finished item to show to Hoffs: "Oh yes, she said, she really liked it... but could we make it in black? It was totally the opposite of what we'd been working on! So we did the next one much quicker," he recalls, "and the limited edition came out in 1988 in black, with checker binding.

"To be honest there was some resistance from heavy metal guys who didn't really want to play a guitar with a woman's name on it," says Davis. "But I think that when people found out what we were trying to do with the guitar, with the pickups and the slightly wider neck, they figured it was an interesting instrument," he says.

In January 1989 Rickenbacker moved the guitar factory from Kilson Drive, after some 27 years at that site, and consolidated factory and offices at the present building on the corner of South Main and Stevens in Santa Ana. The efficiency of the flow of products through the plant was immediately improved, the facilities for paint spraying in particular were upgraded, and in general the new factory was felt to be a far more suitable manufacturing environment. By the early 1990s, on another upward sales curve, Rickenbacker had some 75 people working at the factory, but this was down again to about 60 in 1994.

HEADSTOCK SHAPELINESS

Later in 1989 the company issued a very special group of limited edition models relating to one of the company's most famous players, the late John Lennon. Contact was made with Yoko Ono via her attorney, and in what must have been some delicate negotiations on behalf of Rickenbacker, Davis recalls pointing out that the company wanted to make an authentic tribute to John Lennon. "We said that from a musical

instrument manufacturer's point of view, we would be as sensitive to John Lennon as he was to his music – and that was very sincere, that wasn't bullshit. Anyway, her attorney called back and said yes, they wanted to talk about it."

Once the go-ahead was given, the team at Rickenbacker did some detailed research. John Hall recalls that there was a good deal of to-ing and fro-ing about the exact shape of the headstock. "We found and borrowed a 325 in Los Angeles that was within a few serial numbers of John Lennon's 1963 model. At the factory we had a whole stack of tooling for the head, and we just went through the stack until we matched it." Essentially, Rickenbacker realized that the task involved was much more than merely issuing a 325 with John Lennon's name on it. Accordingly, a large collection of reference material relating to Lennon's 1963 Rickenbacker 325 was accumulated, and after much thought and discussion the company team came up with what one insider refers to as "the most authentic representation of the guitar that John Lennon played".

FROM LENNON TO PETTY

As well as the 'correct' short-scale 325, Rickenbacker also issued full-scale versions of the limited edition, designated 355, and a full-scale 12-string, prompted by a custom 325/12 they'd made for country guitarist John Jorgenson (best known for his work in the Desert Rose Band). Rickenbacker's John Lennon limited edition of 2000 guitars was thus made up of short-scale, full-scale (vibrato and non-vibrato), and full-scale 12-string versions.

Yoko Ono was very particular about the way in which Lennon's image was interpreted, and insisted on an artist's impression rather than a photograph of him being used in advertising and promotional material. The logo on the guitar was a Lennon self-portrait, the same as that used in the film *Imagine* which was released around the same time as the guitars. The launch of the Lennon models gave Rickenbacker a huge amount of publicity from all sections of the media, and there can be little doubt that these guitars did more to raise the awareness of Rickenbacker's instruments than perhaps any other recent model produced by the company.

Tom Petty & The Heartbreakers had long championed the

Rickenbacker cause, and an official association with Petty and the group's lead guitarist Mike Campbell began in 1987 when informal discussions were opened concerning some custom guitars for the two musicians. Dick Burke and Brian Carman subsequently built Petty an unusual *solid maple* old-style 360. This fulfilled Petty's desire for a six-string that looked like the 12-string George Harrison played, as well as one that would not feed back, as the semi-acoustics were prone to do. The disadvantage for Petty was the necessary weightlifting course.

Around 1990 Petty began to talk to Rickenbacker about a 600-style 12-string as a potential instrument for the company's limited edition program. The 'cresting wave' shape of this family of Rickenbackers had been associated with Petty since he had appeared on the cover of his successful *Damn The Torpedoes* album in 1979 with Mike Campbell's 620/12 — which was the solidbody member of the original trio of trial electric 12-strings that Rickenbacker had made back in 1963.

The 660/12TP was launched at the NAMM trade show in 1991, a handsome guitar constructed from selected bird's-eye maple, with checkered binding around the edge of the body, as requested by Petty. One of the most common criticisms of Rickenbacker's 12-string instruments had been that for many guitarists the neck was too narrow, especially at the nut, and that the strings consequently felt too close together. Petty counted himself among these critics; thus he asked for and received a wider neck as standard on the Tom Petty limited edition model.

TAKING THE LEAD

In 1992 John Hall devised a new series of Rickenbackers, the 24-fret 650 series, which share the body style of the earlier 400 and 600 'cresting wave' series. But with their wider necks and high output pickups the 650s are designed to compete with more mainstream instruments. "We've always been criticized for 'only making rhythm guitars'," says John Hall. "Well, these are lead guitars, and that's precisely how they're being marketed by the company."

That same year Hall restyled the 230 Hamburg and 250 El Dorado guitars with slightly wider, satin-finished necks, contouring on the body, a more conventional control circuit,

and the humbucking pickups developed for the John Kay model. A version of the revised Hamburg model provided Rickenbacker with their most recent limited edition model, the 230GF Glenn Frey, derived from what seemed the rather basic requirements of the ex-Eagles musician.

The new models are, Hall explains, a very important part of Rickenbacker's modern business strategy, in parallel with what for want of a better term might be called the company's 'traditional' guitars. "The problem is that throughout the world the production of electric guitars is decreasing very rapidly," Hall explains. "So that means if you're going to grow, it has to be at someone else's expense. That's business. In the past our method had been to carve out new niches, perhaps where business didn't exist before. But now we're street-fighting for that market share."

FROM HAMBURG TO EL DORADO

Forty years after their first two 'modern' electric models appeared, Rickenbacker's 1994 pricelist shows no less than 37 electric guitars, separated into three headings. *Guitars*: 220 Hamburg $899; 260 El Dorado $1049; 610 $999; 610/12 $1099; 620 $1099; 620/12 $1199; 650 Atlantis $1099; 650 Colorado $1099; 650 Dakota $999; 650 Excalibur $1199; 650 Sierra $1099; 330 $1199; 330/12 $1299; 340 $1324; 340/12 $1424; 350 Liverpool $1269; 360 $1319; 360WB $1429; 360/12 $1419; 360/12WB $1529; 370 $1444; 370WB $1554; 370/12 $1544; 370/12WB $1654. *Vintage Reissues*: 325V59 $1659; 325V63 $1659; 350V63 $1689; 350/12V63 $1789; 360V64 $1559; 360/12V64 $1659; 1997 $1429; 1997SPC $1554; 381V69 $2189; 381/12V69 $2289. *Limited Edition*: 230 Glenn Frey $999; 381 John Kay $1799; 660/12 Tom Petty $1699.

Clearly, this represents Rickenbacker's current policy: on one hand they appear to have a sensible and reasonably conscientious attitude to recreating their stylish and distinctive past; on the other hand, there are enough new developments and mainstream designs to satisfy the contemporary guitarist more inclined toward the styles and fashions of the 1990s. Let us hope that the company maintains its desire to produce an intriguing range of guitars that combine the best of past, present and future.

335 prototype c1956 (right) This was an early factory test for the Capri series, launched a few years later. Note the long soundhole, the double carve around the Kauffman vibrato tailpiece, and the twin-knob/twin-switch control layout, all of which were changed on later production versions.

Jackson Browne prototype 1992 (left) Intended as another signature model, this good-looker is based on the requirements of Jackson Browne. It combines the 'cresting wave' styling on a solid body that is equipped with three pickups: two single-coil units and a humbucker in the bridge position. The turquoise blue body is enhanced by the gold plastic two-tier pickguard which carries a simple-looking control layout. The finer design points of this attractive guitar have yet to be finalized between artist and maker.

Astro kit guitar 1963 (left)
The kit of parts could be built up into a very non-Rickenbacker-style, futuristic-looking solid electric, as evidenced by this finished sample.

335 factory experiment 1966
(left) The ungainly looking switch on the oversized pickguard and the huge vibrato unit were designed to provide a transposing function.

System 490 trial 1973 (right)
Devized by John Hall as a 'modular' guitar, the System 490 was intended to have pickup and circuitry modules in a removable pickguard. It never went into production.

First 12-string 1963 (left) This was the very first electric 12-string guitar made by Rickenbacker, given to cabaret artist Suzi Arden in 1963. The instrument's serial number indicates that it was made in July of that year, before Rickenbacker's famous second 12-string – which was later presented to George Harrison during the Beatles' first visit to the United States in February 1964. Harrison's 12-string and all the later versions of the 360/12 were different to this first example, which came with early-style 'oven' knobs, a bound soundhole, and a gold pickguard. However, the flat 'trapeze' tailpiece which originally adorned this unique instrument has at some stage been replaced with a later 'R' type.

REFERENCE
SECTION

REFERENCE SECTION

There are four parts within the reference section that takes up the rest of this book. Starting on this page is the MODEL IDENTIFICATION INDEX, explained below. The main REFERENCE LISTING begins on page 72, and how best to use it is covered on pages 70 and 71. Methods for DATING Rickenbackers, including all-important serial number tables, can be found on pages 88 and 89. Closing the reference section on page 90 is a CHRONOLOGY showing all Rickenbacker electric guitars in the order that they were introduced.
As with any brand, there are exceptions to any 'rules', such as custom order instruments and examples modified by owners, but this reference section will enable you to determine these differences.

THE MODEL IDENTIFICATION INDEX, which commences below and continues to page 69, is designed to help you quickly and simply distinguish between Rickenbacker models. Being able to tell one from another is not always easy as there is usually no indication of a model name or number on the guitar (although some examples do carry the appropriate designation on the truss-rod cover). The first clue is the body shape and there are 15 distinctive designs, which we have chosen to call STYLES, each identified by a number and silhouette. Under every style is a list of the guitars employing that body outline, and each entry gives a brief description of easily recognizable comparative identification features. This is followed by the relevant Rickenbacker model number/name, production period, and a page number indicating where to look in the main Reference Listing for more detailed information.
By first matching a guitar to the correct body silhouette, and then checking the identification features listed under the appropriate style heading, it should be possible to ascertain the model number and its entry in the main Reference Listing.

66

IDENTIFICATION FEATURES	MODEL	MADE	PAGE
STYLE ONE (1932-50) Non-cutaway large body			
F-holes in upper bouts of flat-top wood body	Electro Spanish	1932-35	72
F-holes in lower bouts of flat-top wood body	Ken Roberts	1935-40	72
F-holes in upper bouts of archtop wood body	Spanish (SP)	1946-50	72
F-holes in lower bouts of archtop wood body	S-59	1940-42	72
STYLE TWO (1935-42) Non-cutaway very small body (approx 13 in wide)			
Four chromed plates on front of very small Bakelite body	Vibrola Spanish	1937-42	72
Five chromed or white plates on front of very small Bakelite body	Electro Spanish	1935-42	72
STYLE THREE (1954-59) Offset cutaways (left shallow, right deep) on small body (approx 12³/₄ in wide)			
Two controls, one selector	Combo 600	1954-59	73
Two controls, two selectors	Combo 800	1954-59	73

BODY STYLES
*Each main model entry above
includes a 'Style bar' to identify
which of Rickenbacker's 15
distinctive body Styles is used.
The Styles are shown in silhouette,
on the right, numbered 1 to 15.*

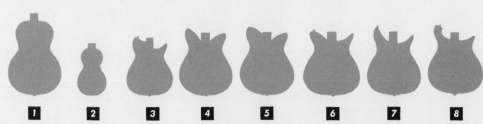

STYLE FOUR (1956-57) Offset cutaways (both curving out, providing 'tulip' shape) on small body (approx 13 in wide)

One pickup, 18 frets	Model 1000	1957	73
One pickup, 21 frets	Combo 400	1956-57	73
Two pickups	Combo 450	1957	73

STYLE FIVE (1957) Offset cutaways (both curving out, but thicker left horn, providing uneven 'tulip' shape) on small body (approx 13 in wide)

One pickup	Model 900	1957	73
Two pickups	Model 950	1957	73

STYLE SIX (1957-71) Offset cutaways (left curving out, right shallow with slight inward curve) on small body (approx 13 in wide)

One pickup at neck	Combo 400	1957-58	74
One pickup near bridge, 18 frets	Model 1000	1957-71	74
One pickup near bridge, 21 frets	Model 900	1957-71	74
Two pickups, short-scale neck	Model 950	1957-71	74
Two pickups, full-scale neck	Combo 450	1957-58	74

STYLE SEVEN (1957-current) Offset cutaways (with pointed horns providing 'sweeping crescent' profile across both) on small body (approx 12¾ in wide)

One pickup, two controls, one selector	Combo 650	1957-59	74
One or two pickups, two controls, two selectors	Combo 850	1957-59	74
Two pickups, short-scale neck, 21 frets	310	1958-71 and 1981-84	74
Two pickups, short-scale neck, 21 frets, vibrato	315	1958-75	75
Three pickups, short-scale neck, 21 frets	320	1958-92	75
Three picjups, short-scale neck, 21 frets, 1960s styling/1980s serial numbers	320B	1983-84	75
Three pickups, short-scale neck, 21 frets, vibrato	325	1958-75 and 1985-92	75
Three pickups, short-scale neck, 21 frets, vibrato, 1960s styling/1980s serial numbers	325B	1983-84	75
Three pickups, short-scale neck, 21 frets, vibrato, 1959 styling/1980s or 1990s serial numbers	325V59	1984-current	75
Three pickups, short-scale neck, 21 frets, vibrato, 1963 styling/1980s or 1990s serial numbers	325V63	1984-current	75
Three pickups, short-scale neck, 21 frets, vibrato, John Lennon signature	325JL	1989-93	75
Three pickups, full-scale neck, 21 frets	350V63	1994-current	76
Three pickups, full-scale neck, 21 frets, John Lennon signature	355JL	1989-93	76
Three pickups, full-scale neck, 21 frets, vibrato, John Lennon signature	355JLVB	1989-93	76
Three pickups, full-scale neck, 24 frets	350	1983-current	75
Three pickups, full-scale neck, 24 frets, Susanna Hoffs signature	350SH	1988-90	76
Three pickups, full-scale neck, 24 frets, vibrato	355	1983-current	76
Three pickups, 12 strings, short-scale neck, 21 frets	325/12	1985-86	75
Three pickups, 12 strings, full-scale neck, 21 frets	350/12V63	1994-current	76
Three pickups, 12 strings, full-scale neck, 21 frets, John Lennon signature	355/12JL	1989-93	76

STYLE EIGHT (1958-current) Offset cutaways (with hooked left horn providing 'cresting wave' across both) on small body (approx 13¼ in wide)

Short-scale neck, one pickup	900	1971-79	78
Short-scale neck, two pickups	950	1971-79	78
One pickup, large pickguard	425	1958-65	76
One pickup, large pickguard	420	1965-83	76
One pickup, large pickguard, vibrato	425	1965-72	76
Two pickups, large pickguard	450	1958-85	77

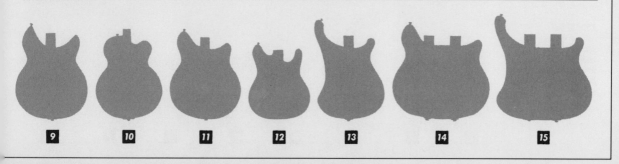

9   10   11   12   13   14   15

IDENTIFICATION FEATURES	MODEL	MADE	PAGE
Two pickups, large pickguard, triangle markers	460	1961-85	77
Two pickups, large pickguard, 12 strings	450/12	1964-85	77
Two pickups, large pickguard, 12 strings,12/6-string converter	456/12	1966-75	77
Two pickups, two-tier pickguard	610	1985-current	77
Two pickups, two-tier pickguard, vibrato	615	1985-current	77
Two pickups, two-tier pickguard, triangle markers	620	1974-current	77
Two pickups, two-tier pickguard, triangle markers, vibrato	625	1962-74 and 1985-current	78
Two pickups, two-tier pickguard, 12 strings	610/12	1988-current	77
Two pickups, two-tier pickguard, 12 strings, triangle markers	620/12	1981-current	78
Two pickups, two-tier pickguard, 12 strings, Tom Petty signature	660/12TP	1991-current	78
24 frets gold hardware	650E	1991-current	78
24 frets, blue body, chrome hardware	650A	1992-current	78
24 frets, black body, chrome hardware	650C	1993-current	78
24 frets, chrome hardware, oiled satin finish	650D	1993-current	78
24 frets, gold hardware, oiled satin finish	650S	1993-current	78

STYLE NINE (1958-current) Offset cutaways (with pointed horns providing 'sweeping crescent' profile across both) on large body (approx 15 in wide)

Two pickups	330	1958-current	79
Two pickups, 1964 UK export style, f-hole/1980s or 1990s serial numbers	1997	1987-current	82
Two pickups, internal lights	331	1970-76	79
Two pickups, vibrato	335	1958-77 and 1985-current	79
Two pickups, vibrato, 1964 UK export style, f-hole/1980s or 1990s serial numbers	1997VB	1987-current	82
Two pickups, triangle markers	360	1958-current	80
Two pickups triangle markers, 1964 styling/1990s serial numbers	360V64	1991-current	80
Two pickups, triangle markers, vibrato	365	1958-76 and 1985-current	80
Two pickups, 12 strings	330/12	1965-current	79
Two pickups, 12 strings, internal lights	331/12	1970-75	79
Two pickups, 12 strings, triangle markers	360/12	1964-current	80
Two pickups, 12 strings, triangle markers, 1964 styling/1980s serial numbers	360/12B WB	1983-84	80
Two pickups, 12 strings, triangle markers, 1964 styling/1980s or 1990s serial numbers	360/12V64	1984-current	80
Two pickups, 12 strings, 12/6-converter	336/12	1966-76	79
Three pickups	340	1958-current	79
Three pickups, 1964 UK export style, f-hole/1990s serial numbers	1997SPC	1992-current	82
Three pickups, Pete Townshend logo	1998PT	1987-88	82
Three pickups, vibrato	345	1958-75 and 1985-current	80
Three pickups, triangle markers	370	1958-current	81
Three pickups, triangle markers, vibrato	375	1958-74 and 1985-current	81
Three pickups, 12 strings	340/12	1980-current	80
Three pickups, 12 strings, triangle markers	370/12	1964-current	81
Body carved front and back, single gold pickguard	381	1958-63	81
Body carved front and back, two-tier white pickguard	381	1969-74	81
Body carved front and back, two-tier white pickguard, 12 strings	381/12	1969-74	82
Body carved front and back, two tier white pickguard, 1969-styling/ 1980s or 1990s serial no's	381V69	1987-current	82
Body carved front and back, two-tier silver pickguard, John Kay signature	381JK	1988-current	82
Body carved front and back, 12 strings	381/12V69	1988-current	82

BODY STYLES
*Each main model entry above
includes a 'Style bar' to identify
which of Rickenbacker's 15
distinctive body Styles is used.
The Styles are shown in silhouette,
on the right, numbered 1 to 15.*

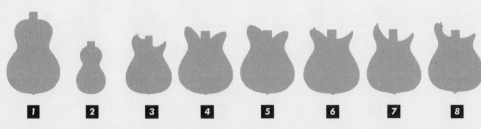

STYLE TEN (1959-80) Shallow right cutaway on large body (approx 17 in wide)

Two pickups, controls on pickguard	330F	1959-67	82
Two pickups, vibrato, controls on pickguard	335F	1959-67	82
Two pickups, triangle markers, controls on pickguard	360F	1959-67	83
Two pickups, triangle markers, controls on body	360F	1968-72	83
Two pickups, triangle markers, vibrato, controls on pickguard	365F	1959-67	83
Two pickups, triangle markers, vibrato, controls on body	365F	1968-72	83
Two pickups, 12 strings	360/12F	1973-80	83
Three pickups, controls on pickguard	340F	1959-67	82
Three pickups, vibrato, controls on pickguard	345F	1959-67	83
Three pickups, triangle markers, controls on pickguard	370F	1959-67	83
Three pickups, triangle markers, controls on body	370F	1968-72	84
Three pickups, triangle markers, vibrato, controls on pickguard	375F	1959-67	84
Three pickups, triangle markers, vibrato, controls on body	375F	1968-72	84

STYLE ELEVEN (1964-current) Offset cutaways (with rounded horns providing 'sweeping crescent' profile across both) on large body (approx 15 in wide)

Two pickups	360	1964-current	84
Two pickups, all-white finish	360SPC Tuxedo	1987	84
Two pickups, vibrato	365	1964-76 and 1985-current	84
Two pickups, 12 strings	360/12	1964-current	84
Two pickups, 12 strings, all white-finish	360/12SPC Tuxedo 12	1987	84
Two pickups, 12 strings, 12/6-string converter	366/12	1966-76	85
Three pickups	370	1964-current	85
Three pickups, vibrato	375	1964-75 and 1985-current	85
Three pickups, 12 strings	370/12	1964-current	85
Three pickups, 12 strings, Roger McGuinn signature	370/12RM	1988-89	85

STYLE TWELVE (1971-current) Offset cutaways with rounded horns on small body (approx 13 in wide)

Rosewood fingerboard, four controls, selector	230	1983-92	86
Rosewood fingerboard, four controls, selector, gold hardware	250	1983-92	86
Rosewood fingerboard, four controls, selector, black pickguard	430	1971-82	86
Maple fingerboard, two controls, selector	220	1992-current	85
Maple fingerboard, two controls, selector, gold hardware	260	1992-current	86
Black fingerboard, two controls, selector, Glenn Frey signature	230GF	1992-current	85

STYLE THIRTEEN (1973-83) Offset cutaways (with hooked long left horn providing 'High cresting wave' profile across both) on small body (approx 13 in wide)

Two pickups	480	1973-83	86
Two pickups, slanted frets	481	1974-83	86
Three pickups	483	1980-83	86

STYLE FOURTEEN (1975-current) Offset cutaways with rounded horns on double neck large body (approx 20¼ in wide)

12-string and six-string guitar necks	362/12	1975-92	86

STYLE FIFTEEN (1975-current) Offset cutaways with hooked long left horn on double neck large body (approx 18½ in wide)

Four-string bass and six-string guitar necks	4080	1975-92	87
Four-string bass and 12-string guitar necks	4080/12	1977-92	87

69

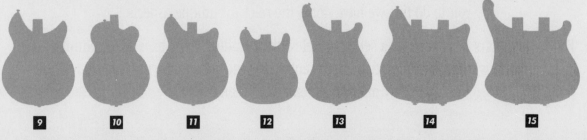

9   10   11   12   13   14   15

REFERENCE LISTING

The main Reference Listing (pages 72-87) uses a simple, condensed format to convey a large amount of information about every Rickenbacker model, and the following notes are intended to ensure that you gain the most from this unique inventory.

The list covers all electric Spanish guitars issued by Rickenbacker between August 1932 and March 1994. Each is allocated to one of 15 distinctive body shapes, called STYLES, which are numbered accordingly in chronological order of introduction. Corresponding body silhouettes are ranged along the bottom of each page, providing an instant and on-going visual reference. Under the style headings the relevant models are listed in numerical sequence, this being necessary due to Rickenbacker's predilection for numbers rather than names – although the latter are also shown where appropriate.

At the head of each entry is the model number designation (and name if applicable) in bold type, followed by a date or range of dates showing the production period of the instrument. These dates and any others in the Reference Section are naturally as accurate as is possible, but should still be considered approximate. As with any other guitar company, there is no guaranteed foolproof method to pinpoint exact periods of manufacture, so all dating should be regarded as a guide, not as gospel.

In italics, following the model number/name and production dates, is a brief, one-sentence identification of the guitar in question. Just as in the preceding Model Identification Index (pages 66-69) this is intended to help you recognize a specific model at a glance. To enable you to do this we have noted the relevant unique aspects.

For some guitars there may be a sentence below this, reading 'As ... except:' or 'Similar to ... except:.' This will refer to another model entry, and the accompanying description will list any major differences between the two.

In most entries there will be a list of specification points, separated into groups, providing details of the model's features. In the order listed the points refer to:

■ Neck, fingerboard, position markers, scale length, frets, headstock.
■ Body, finish.
■ Pickups.
■ Controls; jack socket location.
■ Pickguard.
■ Bridge, tailpiece.
■ Hardware finish.
■ Special features, if any.

Note that various Special Order options were and are available on many models, but not all are recorded in the Reference Listing.

Of course, not every model will need all eight points, and to avoid undue repetition, we have considered a number of features to be common to all Rickenbacker guitars. They are:

Unbound rosewood fingerboard unless stated.

Full scale length 24 ³/₄ in unless stated.

Truss-rod adjustment at headstock unless stated.

Unbound body unless stated.

Nickel- or chrome-plated hardware unless stated.

Some models were made in a number of variations, and where applicable these are listed, in italics, after the specification points. Any other general comments are also made here, in similar fashion.

Some entries comprise only a short listing, all in italics. This is usually because the model concerned is a reissue of, or a re-creation based on, an earlier guitar, and the text simply refers to the original instrument.

Alternative number/name designations are also listed as separate, brief italicized entries. Reading 'See ...,' each refers to the appropriate main model.

All this information is designed to tell you more about your Rickenbacker guitar. By using the general information and illustrations earlier in the book, combined with the knowledge obtained from the Reference Section, you should be able to build up a very full picture of your instrument and its pedigree.

RICKENBACKER REFERENCE LISTING:
ALL ELECTRIC MODELS 1932-1994

STYLE ONE (1932-50)

Non-cutaway large body

ELECTRO SPANISH *1932-35 F-holes in upper bouts of flat-top body.*

Style One

■ Bound fingerboard, dot markers; 25in scale, 19 frets (14 to body); slotted headstock.
■ Hollow flat-top bound body with small f-holes in upper bouts; sunburst.
■ One horseshoe pickup at bridge.
■ No controls (one volume control on body from c1934).
■ Single-saddle wooden bridge, separate trapeze tailpiece.
Neck and body by Harmony, Chicago.

KEN ROBERTS *1935-40 F-holes in lower bouts of flat-top body.*

Style One

■ Bound fingerboard, dot markers; 25in scale, 22 frets (17 to body).
■ Hollow flat-top bound body with f-holes in lower bouts; sunburst.
■ One horseshoe pickup at bridge.
■ One control (volume) on body.
■ Single-saddle bridge, separate vibrato tailpiece.
Neck and body made by Harmony, Chicago.

SPANISH (SP) *1946-50 F-holes in upper bouts of archtop body.*

Style One

■ Bound fingerboard, block markers; 20 frets (14 to body).
■ Hollow archtop bound body with small f-holes in upper bouts; sunburst.
■ One horseshoe pickup at bridge.
■ Two controls (volume, tone) on body.
■ Single-saddle wooden bridge, separate trapeze tailpiece.
Neck and body made by Harmony, Chicago.

S-59 *1940-42 F-holes in lower bouts of archtop body.*

Style One

■ Alternate diamond and twin-dot markers; 19 frets (14 to body).
■ Hollow archtop bound body with f-holes in lower bouts; natural.
■ One narrow horseshoe pickup on body-width bracket near bridge.
■ One control (volume) on pickup bracket.
■ Single-saddle wooden bridge, separate trapeze tailpiece.
Neck and body made by Kay, Chicago.

STYLE TWO (1935-42)

Non-cutaway mini-body

ELECTRO SPANISH *1935-42 Very small black body with five chromed or white plates on front.*

Style Two

■ Bakelite neck; dot markers; 24 frets (14 to body).
■ Bakelite slab body; black.
■ One horseshoe pickup at bridge.
■ One control (volume) on plate (two controls – volume, tone, on two plates from c1938).
■ Five chrome-plated metal plates (white-painted from c1939) on body front.
■ Single-saddle bridge/tailpiece; vibrato tailpiece option.
Known as Model B from c1940.

VIBROLA SPANISH *1937-42 Very small black body with four chromed plates on front.*

Style Two

■ Bakelite neck; dot markers; 24 frets (14 to body).
■ Bakelite slab body; black.
■ One horseshoe pickup at bridge.
■ Two controls (volume, vibrato) on two plates.
■ Four chrome-plated metal plates on body front.

BODY STYLES
Each main model entry above includes a 'Style bar' to identify which of Rickenbacker's 15 distinctive body Styles is used. The Styles are shown in silhouette, on the right, numbered 1 to 15.

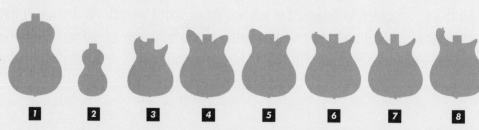

1   2   3   4   5   6   7   8

■ Single-saddle bridge, motorized vibrato tailpiece.

Offset cutaways (left shallow, right deep) on small body

COMBO 600 *1954-59 Two controls and one selector.*

Style Three

■ Bolt-on or glued-in neck; dot markers; 20 frets (21 frets from c1957).
■ Carved-top body; natural or colors.
■ One horseshoe pickup at bridge.
■ Two controls (volume, tone) and three-way selector, all on body (all on elongated pickguard from c1956); side-mounted jack socket.
■ Black plastic pickguard (black or gold plastic elongated pickguard from c1956).
■ Single-saddle bridge/tailpiece with metal cover.

COMBO 800 *1954-59 Two controls and two selectors.*

Style Three

■ Bolt-on or glued-in neck; dot markers; 20 frets (21 frets from c1957).
■ Carved-top body; natural or colors.
■ One horseshoe double pickup at bridge (plus neck pickup from c1957).
■ Two controls (volume, tone) and two three-way selectors, all on body (all on elongated pickguard from c1956); side-mounted jack socket.
■ Black plastic pickguard (black or gold plastic elongated pickguard from c1956).
■ Six-saddle bridge/tailpiece with metal cover.

Offset cutaways (both curving out, providing 'tulip' shape) on small body

COMBO 400 *1956-57 One pickup at neck.*

Style Four

■ Through-neck; dot markers; 21 frets.
■ Solid body; colors.
■ One pickup at neck.
■ Two controls (volume, tone), three-way selector and jack socket, all on pickguard.
■ Anodized metal pickguard.
■ Single-saddle bridge/tailpiece with metal cover.

COMBO 450 *1957 Two pickups.*

Style Four

■ Through-neck; dot markers; 21 frets.
■ Solid body; colors.
■ Two pickups.
■ Two controls (volume, tone), three-way selector and jack socket, all on pickguard.
■ Anodized metal pickguard.
■ Single-saddle bridge/tailpiece with metal cover.

MODEL 1000 *1957 Short-scale neck, 18 frets, one pickup.*

Style Four

■ Through-neck; dot markers; short-scale, 18 frets.
■ Solid body; colors.
■ One pickup near bridge.
■ Two controls (volume, tone), three-way selector and jack socket, all on pickguard.
■ Anodized metal pickguard.

■ Single-saddle bridge/tailpiece with metal cover.

Offset cutaways (both curving out, but thicker left horn providing uneven 'tulip' shape) on small body

MODEL 900 *1957 Short-scale neck, one pickup.*

Style Five

■ Through-neck; dot markers; short-scale, 21 frets.
■ Solid body; colors.
■ One pickup near bridge.
■ Two controls (volume, tone), three-way selector and jack socket, all on pickguard.
■ Anodized metal pickguard.
■ Single-saddle bridge/tailpiece with metal cover.

MODEL 950 *1957 Short-scale neck, two pickups.*

Style Five

■ Through-neck; dot markers; short-scale, 21 frets.
■ Solid body; colors.
■ Two pickups.
■ Two controls (volume, tone), three-way selector and jack socket, all on pickguard.
■ Anodized metal pickguard.
■ Single-saddle bridge/tailpiece with metal cover.

73

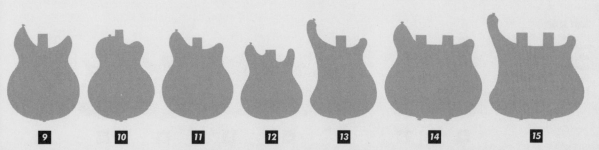

9   10   11   12   13   14   15

STYLE SIX (1957-71)

Offset cutaways (left curving out, right shallow with slight inward curve) on small body

COMBO 400 *1957-58 One pickup at neck.*

Style Six

- Through-neck; dot markers; 21 frets.
- Solid body; colors.
- One pickup at neck.
- Two controls (volume, tone), two three-way selectors and jack socket, all on pickguard.
- Anodized metal pickguard.
- Single-saddle bridge/tailpiece with metal cover.

COMBO 450 *1957-58 Two pickups.*

Style Six

- Through-neck; dot markers; 21 frets.
- Solid body; colors.
- Two pickups.
- Two controls (volume, tone), two three-way selectors and jack socket, all on pickguard.
- Anodized metal pickguard.
- Single-saddle bridge/tailpiece with metal cover.

MODEL 900 *1957-71 Short-scale neck, one pickup near bridge.*

StyleSix

- Glued-in or through-neck; dot markers; short-scale, 21 frets.
- Solid body; colors.
- One pickup near bridge.
- Two controls (volume, tone), two three-way selectors and jack socket, all on pickguard.
- Anodized metal pickguard.

BODY STYLES
Each main model entry above includes a 'Style bar' to identify which of Rickenbacker's 15 distinctive body Styles is used. The Styles are shown in silhouette, on the right, numbered 1 to 15.

- Single-saddle bridge/tailpiece with metal cover.

MODEL 950 *1957-71 Short-scale neck, two pickups.*

Style Six

- Glued-in or through-neck; dot markers; short-scale, 21 frets.
- Solid body; colors.
- Two pickups.
- Two controls (volume, tone), two three-way selectors and jack socket, all on pickguard.
- Anodized metal pickguard.
- Single-saddle bridge/tailpiece with metal cover.

MODEL 1000 *1957-71 Short-scale neck, 18 frets, one pickup near bridge.*

Style Six

- Glued-in or through-neck; dot markers; short-scale, 18 frets.
- Solid body; colors.
- One pickup near bridge.
- Two controls (volume, tone), two three-way selectors and jack socket, all on pickguard.
- Anodized metal pickguard.
- Single-saddle bridge/tailpiece with metal cover.

STYLE SEVEN (1957-current)

Offset cutaways with pointed horns (providing 'sweeping crescent' profile across both) on small body

COMBO 650 *1957-59 Two controls and one selector.*

Style Seven

- Glued-in or through-neck; dot markers; 21 frets.

- Carved-top body; natural or colors.
- One horseshoe pickup at bridge.
- Two controls (volume, tone) and three-way selector, all on pickguard; side-mounted jack socket.
- Gold plastic pickguard.
- Six-saddle bridge/tailpiece with metal cover.

COMBO 850 *1957-59 Two controls and two selectors.*

Style Seven

- Two controls (volume, tone) and two three-way selectors.
- Glued-in or through-neck; dot markers; 21 frets.
- Carved-top body; natural or colors.
- One horseshoe double pickup at bridge (plus neck pickup from c1957).
- Two controls (volume, tone) and two three-way selectors, all on pickguard; side-mounted jack socket.
- Gold plastic pickguard.
- Six-saddle bridge/tailpiece with metal cover.

310 *1958-71 and 1981-84 Short-scale neck, two pickups.*

Style Seven

- Glued-in neck; dot markers; short-scale, 21 frets.
- Semi-acoustic body with or without single soundhole; sunburst, natural or colors.
- Two pickups.
- Four controls (two volume, two tone; fifth control – blend, added from c1963) and three-way selector, all on pickguard; side-mounted jack socket.
- Two-tier gold plastic pickguard (white plastic from c1963).
- Six-saddle bridge, separate tailpiece.
Earliest examples with two controls

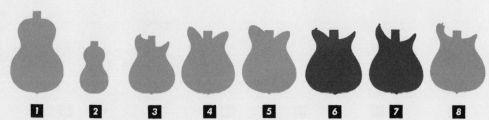

(volume, tone) and three-way selector on single gold plastic pickguard.

315 1958-75 Short-scale neck, two pickups, vibrato tailpiece.

Style Seven

■ Glued-in neck; dot markers; short-scale, 21 frets.
■ Semi-acoustic body with or without single soundhole; sunburst, natural or colors.
■ Two pickups.
■ Four controls (two volume, two tone; fifth control – blend, added from c1963) and three-way selector, all on pickguard; side-mounted jack socket.
■ Two-tier gold plastic pickguard (white plastic from c1963).
■ Six-saddle bridge, separate vibrato tailpiece.
Earliest examples with two controls (volume, tone) and three-way selector on single gold plastic pickguard.

320 1958-1992 Short-scale neck, three pickups.

Style Seven

■ Glued-in neck; dot markers; short-scale, 21 frets.
■ Semi-acoustic body with or without single soundhole; sunburst, natural or colors.
■ Three pickups.
■ Four controls (two volume, two tone; fifth control – blend, added from c1963) and three-way selector, all on pickguard; side-mounted jack socket.
■ Two-tier gold plastic pickguard (white plastic from c1963).
■ Six-saddle bridge, separate tailpiece.
Earliest examples with two controls (volume, tone) and three-way selector on single gold plastic pickguard.

320B 1983-84 Vintage re-issue based on 1960-period four knob original.

320VB See 325 listing.

325 1958-75, 85-92 Short-scale neck, three pickups, vibrato tailpiece.

Style Seven

■ Glued-in neck; dot markers; short-scale, 21 frets.
■ Semi-acoustic body with or without single soundhole; sunburst, natural or colors.
■ Three pickups.
■ Four controls (two volume, two tone; fifth control – blend, added from c1963) and three-way selector, all on pickguard; side-mounted jack socket.
■ Two-tier gold plastic pickguard (white plastic from c1963).
■ Six-saddle bridge, separate vibrato tailpiece.
Earliest examples with two controls (volume, tone) and three-way selector on single gold plastic pickguard.
325S export version known as Model 1996 in UK 1964-67.
320VB with vibrato tailpiece option (thus 325 specification) from 1985.

325B 1983-84 Vintage re-issue based on 1960-period four knob original.

325JL JOHN LENNON 1989-93 Signature on pickguard, short-scale, vibrato tailpiece.

Style Seven

■ Glued-in neck; dot markers; short-scale, 21 frets.
■ Semi-acoustic body; black only.
■ Three pickups.
■ Five controls (two volume, two tone, one blend) and three-way selector, all on pickguard; side-mounted jack socket.
■ Two-tier white plastic pickguard.
■ Six-saddle bridge, separate vibrato tailpiece.
■ John Lennon signature, 'Limited Edition' and Lennon drawing on pickguard.
Limited edition of 953, plus 21 left-hand examples.

325V59 1984-current Vintage re-issue based on 1959-period four knob original.

325V63 1984-current Vintage re-issue based on 1963-period five knob original.

325/12 1985-86 12 strings, short-scale neck, three pickups.

Style Seven

■ Glued-in neck; dot markers; short-scale, 21 frets; 12-string headstock.
■ Semi-acoustic body with or without single soundhole; sunburst, natural or colors.
■ Three pickups.
■ Five controls (two volume, two tone, one blend) and three-way selector, all on pickguard; side-mounted jack socket.
■ Two-tier white plastic pickguard.
■ Six-saddle bridge, separate tailpiece.

350 LIVERPOOL 1983-current 24 frets, three pickups.

Style Seven

■ Glued-in neck; dot markers; 24 frets.
■ Semi-acoustic body with no soundhole; sunburst, natural or colors.
■ Three pickups.
■ Five controls (two volume, two tone,

75

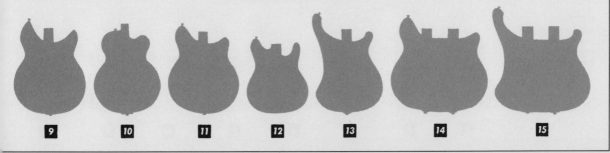

9   10   11   12   13   14   15

one blend) and three-way selector, all on pickguard; side-mounted jack socket.
- Two-tier white plastic pickguard.
- Six-saddle bridge, separate tailpiece.

350SH SUSANNA HOFFS *1988-90 24 frets, signature on pickguard.*

Style Seven

- Glued-in neck with bound fingerboard, triangle markers; 24 frets.
- Semi-acoustic bound body; black only.
- Three pickups, humbucker at bridge.
- Five controls (two volume, two tone, one blend) and three-way selector, all on pickguard; side-mounted jack socket.
- Two-tier white plastic pickguard.
- Six-saddle bridge, separate tailpiece.
- Susanna Hoffs signature and 'Limited Edition' on pickguard.
Limited edition of 246, plus 4 left-hand examples.

350VB LIVERPOOL *See 355 Liverpool Plus listing.*

350V63 *1994-current Signature-less version of 355JL John Lennon discontinued in 1993.*

350/12V63 *1994-current Signature-less version of 355/12JL John Lennon 12-string discontinued in 1993.*

355 LIVERPOOL PLUS *1983-current 24 frets, three pickups, vibrato tailpiece.*

Style Seven

- Glued-in neck; dot markers; 24 frets.
- Semi-acoustic body with no soundhole; sunburst, natural or colors.
- Three pickups.

Five controls (two volume, two tone, one blend) and three-way selector, all on pickguard; side-mounted jack socket.
- Two-tier white plastic pickguard.
- Six-saddle bridge, separate vibrato tailpiece.
350VB with vibrato tailpiece option (thus 355 specification) from 1985.

355JL JOHN LENNON *1989-93 Signature on pickguard, full-scale, non-vibrato tailpiece.*

Style Seven

- Glued-in neck; dot markers; 21 frets.
- Semi-acoustic body; black only.
- Three pickups.
- Five controls (two volume, two tone, one blend) and three-way selector, all on pickguard; side-mounted jack socket.
- Two-tier white plastic pickguard.
- Six-saddle bridge, separate tailpiece.
- John Lennon signature, 'Limited Edition' and Lennon drawing on pickguard.
Limited edition of 660, plus 8 left-hand examples.

355JLVB JOHN LENNON *1989-93 Signature on pickguard, full-scale, vibrato tailpiece.*
As 355JL, except:
- Vibrato tailpiece.
Limited edition of 23.

355/12JL JOHN LENNON *1989-93 12 strings, signature on pickguard.*

Style Seven

- Glued-in neck; dot markers; 21 frets; 12-string headstock.
- Semi-acoustic body; black only.

- Three pickups.
- Five controls (two volume, two tone, one blend) and three-way selector, all on pickguard; side-mounted jack socket.
- Two-tier white plastic pickguard.
- Six-saddle bridge, separate tailpiece.
- John Lennon signature, 'Limited Edition' and Lennon drawing on pickguard.
Limited edition of 329, plus 5 left-hand examples.

'1996' *See 325 listing.*

STYLE EIGHT (1958-current)

Offset cutaways (with hooked left horn providing 'cresting wave' profile across both) on small body

420 *1965-83 One pickup, large single pickguard.*

Style Eight

- Glued-in or through-neck; dot markers; 21 frets.
- Solid body; sunburst, natural or colors.
- One pickup at bridge.
- Two controls (volume, tone), three-way selector and jack socket, all on pickguard.
- White plastic pickguard.
- Single-saddle bridge/tailpiece.
Replaced non-vibrato 425 from 1965.

425 *1958-72 One pickup, large single pickguard.*

Style Eight

- Glued-in or through-neck; dot markers; 21 frets.
- Solid body; sunburst, natural or colors.

76

BODY STYLES
Each main model entry above includes a 'Style bar' to identify which of Rickenbacker's 15 distinctive body Styles is used. The Styles are shown in silhouette, on the right, numbered 1 to 15.

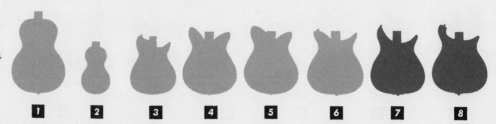

1 2 3 4 5 6 7 8

■ One pickup at bridge.
■ Two controls (volume, tone), three-way selector and jack socket, all on pickguard.
■ White plastic pickguard.
■ Single-saddle bridge/tailpiece (vibrato tailpiece from 1965).
Non-vibrato 425 replaced by 420 from 1965.

450 *1958-85 Two pickups, large single pickguard.*

Style Eight

■ Glued-in or through-neck; dot markers; 21 frets.
■ Solid body; sunburst, natural or colors.
■ Two pickups.
■ Four controls (two volume, two tone), three-way selector and jack socket, all on pickguard.
■ Anodized metal pickguard (white plastic from c1962).
■ Six-saddle bridge/tailpiece with metal cover (single-saddle bridge/tailpiece from c1964).
Earliest examples with two controls (volume, tone) and two three-way selectors.

450/12 *1964-85 12 strings, two pickups, large single pickguard.*

Style Eight

■ Through-neck; dot markers; 21 frets; 12-string headstock.
■ Solid body; sunburst, natural or colors.
■ Two pickups.
■ Four controls (two volume, two tone), three-way selector and jack socket, all on pickguard.
■ White plastic pickguard.
■ Single-saddle bridge/tailpiece.

456/12 *1966-75 12 strings, two pickups, 12/6-string converter unit.*
As 450/12, except:
■ 12/6-string converter unit mounted on body.

460 *1961-85 Triangle markers, two pickups, large single pickguard.*

Style Eight

■ Through-neck with bound fingerboard, triangle markers; 21 frets.
■ Solid bound body; sunburst, natural or colors.
■ Two pickups.
■ Five controls (two volume, two tone, one blend) and three-way selector, all on pickguard; side-mounted jack socket(s).
■ Anodized metal pickguard (white plastic from c1962).
■ Six-saddle bridge/tailpiece with metal cover (single-saddle bridge/tailpiece from c1964).

610 *1985-current Two pickups, two-tier pickguard.*

Style Eight

■ Through-neck; dot markers; 21 frets.
■ Solid body; sunburst, natural or colors.
■ Two pickups.
■ Five controls (two volume, two tone, blend) and three-way selector, all on pickguard; side-mounted jack socket.
■ Two-tier white plastic pickguard.
■ Six-saddle bridge, separate tailpiece.

610VB *See 615 listing.*

610/12 *1988-current 12 strings, two pickups, two-tier pickguard.*

Style Eight

■ Through-neck; dot markers; 21 frets; 12-string headstock.
■ Solid body; sunburst, natural or colors.
■ Two pickups.
■ Five controls (two volume, two tone, blend) and three-way selector, all on pickguard; side-mounted jack socket.
■ Two-tier white plastic pickguard.
■ Six-saddle bridge, separate tailpiece.

615 *1962-74 and 1985-current Two pickups, two-tier pickguard, vibrato tailpiece.*

Style Eight

■ Through-neck; dot markers; 21 frets.
■ Solid body; sunburst, natural or colors.
■ Two pickups.
■ Four controls (two volume, two tone; fifth control – blend, added from c1963) and three-way selector, all on pickguard; side-mounted jack socket.
■ Two-tier white plastic pickguard.
■ Six-saddle bridge, separate vibrato tailpiece.
Earliest examples with gold plastic pickguard.
615S export version known as Model 1995 in UK 1964.
610VB with vibrato tailpiece option (thus 615 specification) from 1985.

620 *1974-current Triangle markers, two pickups, two-tier pickguard.*

Style Eight

■ Through-neck with bound fingerboard, triangle markers, 21 frets.
■ Solid bound body; sunburst, natural or colors.
■ Two pickups.
■ Five controls (two volume, two tone, one blend) and three-way selector, all

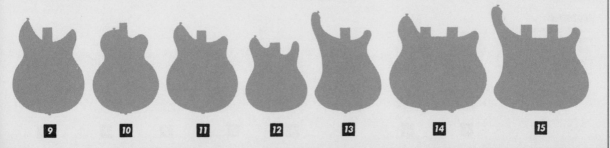

9   10   11   12   13   14   15

77

on pickguard; side-mounted jack sockets.
■ Two-tier white plastic pickguard.
■ Six-saddle bridge, separate tailpiece.

620VB See 625 listing.

620/12 *1981-current 12 strings, triangle markers, two pickups, two-tier pickguard.*

Style Eight

■ Through-neck with bound fingerboard, triangle markers, 21 frets; 12-string headstock.
■ Solid bound body; sunburst, natural or colors.
■ Two pickups.
■ Five controls (two volume, two tone, one blend) and three-way selector, all on pickguard; side-mounted jack sockets.
■ Two-tier white plastic pickguard.
■ Six-saddle bridge, separate tailpiece.

625 *1962-74 and 1985-current Triangle markers, two pickups, two-tier pickguard, vibrato tailpiece.*

Style Eight

■ Through-neck with bound fingerboard, triangle markers, 21 frets.
■ Solid bound body; sunburst, natural or colors.
■ Two pickups.
■ Five controls (two volume, two tone, one blend) and three-way selector, all on pickguard; side-mounted jack sockets.
■ Two-tier white plastic pickguard.
■ Six-saddle bridge, separate vibrato tailpiece.
620VB with vibrato tailpiece option (thus 625 specification) from 1985.

650A ATLANTIS *1992-current Maple through-neck, 24 frets, blue body wings, chrome-plated hardware.*

Style Eight

■ All-maple through-neck; dot markers; 24 frets.
■ Solid body; blue maple wings.
■ Two pickups.
■ Four controls (two volume, two tone) and three-way selector, all on pickguard; side-mounted jack socket.
■ Chrome-plated metal pickguard.
■ Six-saddle bridge, through-body stringing; vibrato option from 1994.

650C COLORADO *1993-current Maple through-neck, 24 frets, all-black body, chrome-plated hardware.*
As 650A Atlantis, except:
■ Black body, neck and headstock.

650D DAKOTA *1993-current Maple through-neck, 24 frets, walnut brown body wings, chrome-plated hardware.*
As 650A Atlantis, except:
■ Headstock laminated with contrasting wood (walnut).
■ Natural walnut wings.
■ Oiled satin finish.

650E EXCALIBUR *1991-current Maple through-neck, 24 frets, vermilion brown body wings, gold-plated hardware.*
As 650A Atlantis, except:
■ Headstock laminated with contrasting wood (vermilion).
■ Natural vermilion wings.
■ Gold-plated hardware.

650S SIERRA *1993-current Maple through-neck, 24 frets, dark walnut brown body wings, gold-plated hardware.*

As 650A Atlantis, except:
■ Headstock laminated with contrasting wood (dark walnut).
■ Natural dark walnut wings.
■ Gold-plated hardware.
■ Oiled satin finish.

660/12TP TOM PETTY *1991-current 12 strings, signature on pickguard.*

Style Eight

■ Through-neck with bound fingerboard, triangle markers.
■ Solid bound body; sunburst or black.
■ Two pickups.
■ Five controls (two volume, two tone, blend) and three-way selector, all on pickguard; side-mounted jack socket.
■ Two-tier gold plastic pickguard.
■ 12-saddle bridge, separate flat trapeze tailpiece.
■ Tom Petty signature and 'Limited Edition' on pickguard.
Limited edition of 1000.

900 *1971-79 Short-scale neck, one pickup, large single pickguard.*

Style Eight

■ Glued-in neck; dot markers; short-scale, 21 frets.
■ Solid body; sunburst, natural or colors.
■ One pickup.
■ Two controls (volume, tone), three-way selector and jack socket, all on pickguard.
■ White plastic pickguard.
■ Single-saddle bridge/tailpiece.

950 *1971-79 Short-scale neck, two pickups, large single pickguard.*

Style Eight

BODY STYLES
Each main model entry above includes a 'Style bar' to identify which of Rickenbacker's 15 distinctive body Styles is used. The Styles are shown in silhouette, on the right, numbered 1 to 15.

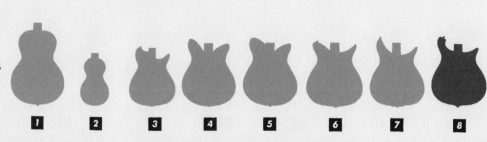

1 2 3 4 5 6 7 8

78

■ Glued-in neck; dot markers; short-scale, 21 frets.
■ Solid body; sunburst, natural or colors.
■ Two pickups.
■ Four controls (two volume, two tone), three-way selector and jack socket, all on pickguard.
■ White plastic pickguard.
■ Single-saddle bridge/tailpiece.

'1995' See 615 listing.

STYLE NINE (1958-current)

Offset cutaways (with pointed horns providing 'sweeping crescent' profile across both) on large body

330 1958-current Two pickups.

Style Nine

■ Glued-in neck; dot markers; 21 frets (24 frets phased in from c1969).
■ Semi-acoustic body with single soundhole; sunburst, natural or colors.
■ Two pickups.
■ Four controls (two volume, two tone; fifth control – blend, added from c1963) and three-way selector, all on pickguard; side-mounted jack socket.
■ Two-tier gold plastic pickguard (white plastic from c1963).
■ Six-saddle bridge, separate tailpiece.
Earliest examples with two controls (volume, tone) and one or two three-way selectors on single gold plastic pickguard.

330VB See 335 listing.

330/12 1965-current 12 strings, two pickups.

Style Nine

■ Glued-in neck; dot markers; 21 frets (24 frets phased in from c1969); 12-string headstock.
■ Semi-acoustic body with single soundhole; sunburst, natural or colors.
■ Two pickups.
■ Five controls (two volume, two tone, one blend) and three-way selector, all on pickguard; side-mounted jack socket.
■ Two-tier white plastic pickguard.
■ Six-saddle bridge, separate tailpiece.
330S/12 export version known as Model 1993 in UK 1964-67.

331 'LIGHT SHOW' 1970-76 Translucent plastic body front displaying internal lighting.

Style Nine

■ Glued-in neck with bound fingerboard, dot markers; 24 frets.
■ Semi-acoustic body with translucent plastic sectioned front.
■ Two pickups.
■ Six controls (two volume, two tone, one blend, one light dimmer) and three-way selector, all on body front.
■ Six-saddle bridge, separate tailpiece.
■ Internal lights and circuitry, external power supply.
Earliest examples use straight rows of white lights fitted with colored filters, later versions have staggered, colored lights.

331/12 'LIGHT SHOW' 1970-75 12 strings, translucent plastic body front displaying internal lighting.
As 331, except:
■ 12-string headstock.

335 1958-77 and 1985-current Two pickups, vibrato tailpiece.

Style Nine

■ Glued-in neck; dot markers; 21 frets (24 frets phased in from c1969).
■ Semi-acoustic body with single soundhole; sunburst, natural or colors.
■ Two pickups.
■ Four controls (two volume, two tone; fifth control – blend, added from c1963) and three-way selector, all on pickguard; side-mounted jack socket.
■ Two-tier gold plastic pickguard (white plastic from c1963).
■ Six-saddle bridge, separate vibrato tailpiece.
Earliest examples with two controls (volume, tone) and one or two three-way selectors on single gold plastic pickguard.
335S export version known as Model 1997 in UK 1964-68.
330VB with vibrato tailpiece option (thus 335 specification) from 1985.

336/12 1966-76 12 strings, two pickups, 12/6-string converter unit.
As 330/12, except:
■ 12/6-string converter unit mounted on body.
336S/12 export version, known as Model 3262 in UK 1967.

340 1958-current Three pickups.

Style Nine

■ Glued-in neck; dot markers; 21 frets (24 frets phased in from c1969).
■ Semi-acoustic body with single soundhole; sunburst, natural or colors.
■ Three pickups.
■ Four controls (two volume, two tone; fifth control – blend, added from

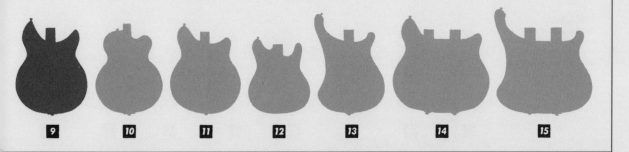

9   10   11   12   13   14   15

c1963) and three-way selector, all on pickguard; side-mounted jack socket.
■ Two-tier gold plastic pickguard (white plastic from c1963).
■ Six-saddle bridge, separate tailpiece. *Earliest examples with two controls (volume, tone) and one or two three-way selectors on single gold plastic pickguard.*

340VB See 345 listing.

340/12 *1980-current 12 strings, three pickups.*

Style Nine

■ Glued-in neck; dot markers; 24 frets; 12-string headstock.
■ Semi-acoustic body with single soundhole; sunburst, natural or colors.
■ Three pickups.
■ Five controls (two volume, two tone, one blend) and three-way selector, all on pickguard; side-mounted jack socket.
■ Two-tier white plastic pickguard.
■ Six-saddle bridge, separate tailpiece.

345 *1958-75 and 1985-current Three pickups, vibrato tailpiece.*

Style Nine

■ Glued-in neck; dot markers; 21 frets (24 frets phased in from c1969).
■ Semi-acoustic body with single soundhole; sunburst, natural or colors.
■ Three pickups.
■ Four controls (two volume, two tone; fifth control – blend, added from c1963) and three-way selector, all on pickguard; side-mounted jack socket.
■ Two-tier gold plastic pickguard (white plastic from c1963).
■ Six-saddle bridge, separate vibrato tailpiece.

Earliest examples with two controls (volume, tone) and one or two three-way selectors on single gold plastic pickguard.
345S export version known as Model 1998 in UK 1964-67.
340VB vibrato tailpiece option (thus 345 specification) from 1985.

360 *1958-current Triangle markers, two pickups.*

Style Nine

■ Glued-in neck with bound fingerboard, triangle markers; 21 frets (24 frets phased in from c1969).
■ Semi-acoustic bound body with single soundhole; sunburst, natural or colors.
■ Two pickups.
■ Four controls (two volume, two tone; fifth control – blend, added from c1963) and three-way selector, all on pickguard; side-mounted jack socket(s).
■ Two-tier gold plastic pickguard (white plastic from c1963).
■ Six saddle bridge, separate tailpiece.

Earliest examples with two controls (volume, tone) and one or two three-way selectors on single gold plastic pickguard.
SO (Special Order) examples available 1964-84.
360WB from 1984.

360V64 *1991-current Vintage re-issue based on 1964-period original.*

360WB See 360 listing.

360WBVB See 365 listing.

360/12 *1964-current 12 strings, triangle markers, two pickups.*

Style Nine

■ Glued-in neck with bound fingerboard, triangle markers; 21 frets (24 frets phased in from c1969); 12-string headstock.
■ Semi-acoustic bound body with single soundhole; sunburst, natural or colors.
■ Two pickups.
■ Five controls (two volume, two tone, one blend) and three-way selector, all on pickguard; side-mounted jack sockets.
■ Two-tier white plastic pickguard.
■ Six-saddle bridge, separate tailpiece.
360/12 OS from 1964, later changed to 360/12 WBBS, until 1984.
360/12WB from 1984.

360/12B WB *1983-84 Vintage re-issue based on 1964-period original.*

360/12V64 *1984-current Vintage re-issue based on 1964-period original.*

360/12WB See 360/12 listing.

365 *1958-76 and 1985-current Triangle markers, two pickups, vibrato tailpiece.*

Style Nine

■ Glued-in neck with bound fingerboard, triangle markers; 21 frets (24 frets phased in from c1969).
■ Semi-acoustic bound body with single soundhole; sunburst, natural or colors.
■ Two pickups.
■ Four controls (two volume, two tone; fifth control – blend, added from c1963) and three-way selector, all on pickguard; side-mounted jack socket(s).
■ Two-tier gold plastic pickguard (white plastic from c1963).

80

BODY STYLES
Each main model entry above includes a 'Style bar' to identify which of Rickenbacker's 15 distinctive body Styles is used. The Styles are shown in silhouette, on the right, numbered 1 to 15.

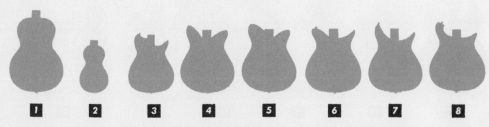

■ Six saddle bridge, separate vibrato tailpiece.
Earliest examples with two controls (volume, tone) and one or two three-way selectors on single gold plastic pickguard.
SO (Special Order) examples available from 1964.
360WBVB with vibrato tailpiece option (thus 365 specification) from 1985.

370 *1958-current Triangle markers, three pickups.*

Style Nine

■ Glued-in neck with bound fingerboard, triangle markers; 21 frets (24 frets phased in from c1969).
■ Semi-acoustic bound body with single soundhole; sunburst, natural or colors.
■ Three pickups.
■ Four controls (two volume, two tone; fifth control – blend, added from c1963) and three-way selector, all on pickguard; side-mounted jack socket(s).
■ Two-tier gold plastic pickguard (white plastic from c1963).
■ Six saddle bridge, separate tailpiece.
Earliest examples with two controls (volume, tone) and one or two three-way selectors on single gold plastic pickguard.
SO (Special Order) examples available 1964-84.
Available as 370WB or as 360WB with third pickup option (thus 370WB specification) from 1984.

370WB See 370 listing.

370WBVB See 375 listing.

370/12 *1964-current 12 strings, triangle markers, three pickups.*

Style Nine

■ Glued-in neck with bound fingerboard, triangle markers; 21 frets (24 frets phased in from c1969); 12-string headstock.
■ Semi-acoustic bound body with single soundhole; sunburst, natural or colors.
■ Three pickups.
■ Five controls (two volume, two tone, one blend) and three-way selector, all on pickguard; side-mounted jack sockets.
■ Six-saddle bridge, separate tailpiece.
Designated 370/12 OS from 1964, later changed to 370/12 WBBS, until 1984. Available as 370/12WB or as 360/12WB with third pickup option (thus 370/12WB specification) from 1984.

370/12WB See 370/12 listing.

375 *1958-74 and 1985-current Triangle markers, three pickups, vibrato tailpiece.*

Style Nine

■ Glued-in neck with bound fingerboard, triangle markers; 21 frets.
■ Semi-acoustic bound body with single soundhole; sunburst, natural or colors.
■ Three pickups.
■ Four controls (two volume, two tone; fifth control – blend, added from c1963) and three-way selector, all on pickguard; side-mounted jack socket(s).
■ Two-tier gold plastic pickguard (white plastic from c1963).
■ Six saddle bridge, separate vibrato tailpiece.

Earliest examples with two controls (volume, tone) and one or two three-way selectors on single gold plastic pickguard.
SO (Special Order) examples available from 1964.
370WBVB with vibrato tailpiece option (thus 375 specification) from 1985.

381 'first version' *1958-63 Hollow carved deep body, single gold plastic pickguard.*

Style Nine

■ Glued-in neck with bound fingerboard, triangle markers; 21 frets.
■ Hollow, carved-top and back bound body with single soundhole; sunburst or natural.
■ Two pickups.
■ Two controls (volume, tone) and two three-way selectors, all on pickguard; side-mounted jack socket(s).
■ Gold plastic pickguard.
■ Six-saddle bridge, separate tailpiece.
Some early examples with dot fingerboard markers.

381 'second version' *1969-74 Hollow carved deep body, two-tier white plastic pickguard.*

Style Nine

■ Glued-in neck with bound fingerboard, triangle markers; 21 frets.
■ Hollow, carved-top and back bound body with single soundhole; sunburst, natural or colors.
■ Two pickups.
■ Five controls (two volume, two tone, one blend) and three-way selector, all on pickguard; side-mounted jack socket(s).
■ Two-tier white plastic pickguard.

81

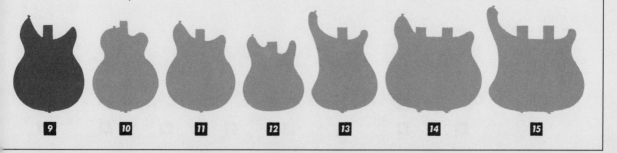

9   10   11   12   13   14   15

■ Six-saddle bridge, separate tailpiece.

381/12 *1969-74 12 strings, hollow carved deep body, two-tier white plastic pickguard.*
As 381 'second version', except:
■ 12-string headstock.

381JK JOHN KAY *1988-current Signature on pickguard.*

Style Nine

■ Glued-in neck with bound fingerboard, triangle markers; 21 frets.
■ Hollow, carved-top and back bound body with single soundhole; black only.
■ Two humbucker pickups.
■ Five controls (three volume, one tone, one four-way rotary selector), three-way selector and phase mini-switch, all on pickguard; side-mounted jack sockets; active circuit.
■ Two-tier silver plastic pickguard.
■ Six-saddle bridge, separate tailpiece.
■ John Kay signature, 'Limited Edition' and 'Steppenwolf' logo on pickguard.
Limited edition of 250.

381V69 *1987-current Vintage re-issue based on 1969-period original.*

381/12V69 *1988-current 12 strings, hollow carved deep body.*
As 381V69, except:
■ 12-string headstock.
■ 12-saddle bridge.
Vintage re-issue based on small production 1969-period original.

'1993' See 330/12 listing.

'1997' See 335 listing.

1997 *1987-current Vintage re-issue supposedly based on 1964-period export version of the 335, but the vibrato tailpiece is absent, making it a 330, which was not the equivalent of the original UK Model 1997. Also 1997SPC with three pickups (1992-current).*

1997VB *1987-current Vintage re-issue based on the 1964-period export version of the 335, complete with correct vibrato tailpiece.*

'1998' See 345 listing.

1998PT PETE TOWNSHEND *1987-88 'Pete Townshend' on pickguard.*

Style Nine

■ Glued-in neck; dot markers; 21 frets.
■ Semi-acoustic body with single soundhole; sunburst only.
■ Three pickups.
■ Five controls (two volume, two tone, one blend) and three-way selector, all on pickguard; side-mounted jack socket.
■ Two-tier white plastic pickguard.
■ Six-saddle bridge, separate tailpiece.
■ 'Pete Townshend Limited Edition' on pickguard.
Limited edition of 250.
Model designation refers to 1960s UK number for export version of the 345, but absence of a vibrato tailpiece makes it a 340, not the correct equivalent of the original Model 1998.

'3262' See 336/12 listing.

Shallow right cutaway on large body

330F *1959-67 Two pickups.*

Style Ten

■ Glued-in neck; dot markers; 21 frets.
■ Semi-acoustic body with single soundhole; sunburst or natural.
■ Two pickups.
■ Four controls (two volume, two tone; fifth control – blend, added from c1963) and three-way selector, all on pickguard; side-mounted jack socket.
■ Two-tier gold plastic pickguard (white plastic from c1963).
■ Six-saddle bridge, separate tailpiece.

335F *1959-67 Two pickups, vibrato tailpiece.*

Style Ten

■ Glued-in neck; dot markers; 21 frets.
■ Semi-acoustic body with single soundhole; sunburst or natural.
■ Two pickups.
■ Four controls (two volume, two tone; fifth control – blend, added from c1963) and three-way selector, all on pickguard; side-mounted jack socket.
■ Two-tier gold plastic pickguard (white plastic from c1963).
■ Six-saddle bridge, separate vibrato.

340F *1959-67 Three pickups.*

Style Ten

■ Glued-in neck; dot markers; 21 frets.
■ Semi-acoustic body with single soundhole; sunburst or natural.
■ Three pickups.
■ Four controls (two volume, two tone; fifth control – blend, added from c1963) and three-way selector, all on pickguard; side-mounted jack socket.

82

BODY STYLES
Each main model entry above includes a 'Style bar' to identify which of Rickenbacker's 15 distinctive body Styles is used. The Styles are shown in silhouette, on the right, numbered 1 to 15.

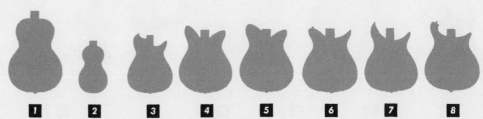

■ Two-tier gold plastic pickguard (white plastic from c1963).
■ Six-saddle bridge, separate tailpiece.

345F 1959-67 *Three pickups, vibrato tailpiece.*

Style Ten

■ Glued-in neck; dot markers; 21 frets.
■ Semi-acoustic body with single soundhole; sunburst or natural.
■ Three pickups.
■ Four controls (two volume, two tone; fifth control – blend, added from c1963) and three-way selector, all on pickguard; side-mounted jack socket.
■ Two-tier gold plastic pickguard (white plastic from c1963).
■ Six-saddle bridge, separate vibrato tailpiece.

360F 'first version' 1959-67 *Triangle markers, two pickups, controls on pickguard.*

Style Ten

■ Glued-in neck with bound fingerboard, triangle markers; 21 frets.
■ Semi-acoustic bound body with single soundhole; sunburst or natural.
■ Two pickups.
■ Four controls (two volume, two tone; fifth control – blend, added from c1963) and three-way selector, all on pickguard; side-mounted jack socket(s).
■ Two-tier gold plastic pickguard (white plastic from c1963).
■ Six-saddle bridge, separate tailpiece.

360F 'second version' 1968-72 *Triangle markers, two pickups, controls on body.*

Style Ten

■ Glued-in neck with bound

fingerboard, triangle markers; 21 frets.
■ Semi-acoustic bound body with single soundhole; sunburst or natural.
■ Two pickups.
■ Five controls (two volume, two tone, one blend) and three-way selector, all on body front; side-mounted jack sockets.
■ White plastic pickguard.
■ Six-saddle bridge, separate tailpiece.

360/12F 1973-80 *12 strings, triangle markers, two pickups, controls on body.*

Style Ten

■ Glued-in neck with bound fingerboard, triangle markers; 21 frets; 12-string headstock.
■ Semi-acoustic bound body with single soundhole; sunburst or natural.
■ Two pickups.
■ Five controls (two volume, two tone, one blend) and three-way selector, all on body front; side-mounted jack sockets.
■ White plastic pickguard.
■ Six-saddle bridge, separate tailpiece. *Also earlier examples built to special order.*

365F 'first version' 1959-67 *Triangle markers, two pickups, controls on pickguard, vibrato tailpiece.*

Style Ten

■ Glued-in neck with bound fingerboard, triangle markers; 21 frets.
■ Semi-acoustic bound body with single soundhole; sunburst or natural.
■ Two pickups.
■ Four controls (two volume, two tone; fifth control – blend, added from c1963) and three-way selector, all on pickguard; side-mounted jack socket(s).

■ Two-tier gold plastic pickguard (white plastic from c1963).
■ Six-saddle bridge, separate vibrato tailpiece.

365F 'second version' 1968-72 *Triangle markers, two pickups, controls on body, vibrato tailpiece.*

Style Ten

■ Glued-in neck with bound fingerboard, triangle markers; 21 frets.
■ Semi-acoustic bound body with single soundhole; sunburst or natural.
■ Two pickups.
■ Five controls (two volume, two tone, one blend) and three-way selector, all on body front; side-mounted jack sockets.
■ White plastic pickguard.
■ Six-saddle bridge, separate vibrato tailpiece.

370F 'first version' 1959-67 *Triangle markers, three pickups, controls on pickguard.*

Style Ten

■ Glued-in neck with bound fingerboard, triangle markers; 21 frets.
■ Semi-acoustic bound body with single soundhole; sunburst or natural.
■ Three pickups.
■ Four controls (two volume, two tone; fifth control – blend, added from c1963) and three-way selector, all on pickguard; side-mounted jack socket(s).
■ Two-tier gold plastic pickguard (white plastic from c1963).
■ Six-saddle bridge, separate tailpiece.

83

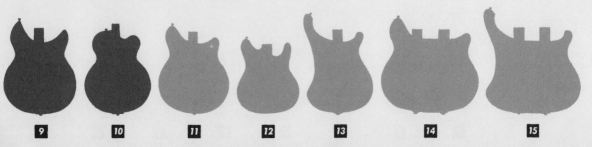

9   10   11   12   13   14   15

370F 'second version' *1968-72 Triangle markers, three pickups, controls on body.*

Style Ten

■ Glued-in neck with bound fingerboard, triangle markers; 21 frets.
■ Semi-acoustic bound body with single soundhole; sunburst or natural.
■ Three pickups.
■ Five controls (two volume, two tone, one blend) and three-way selector, all on body front; side-mounted jack sockets.
■ White plastic pickguard.
■ Six-saddle bridge, separate tailpiece.

375F 'first version' *1959-67 Triangle markers, three pickups, controls on body, vibrato tailpiece.*

Style Ten

■ Glued-in neck with bound fingerboard, triangle markers; 21 frets.
■ Semi-acoustic bound body with single soundhole; sunburst or natural.
■ Three pickups.
■ Four controls (two volume, two tone; fifth control – blend, added from c1963) and three-way selector, all on pickguard; side-mounted jack socket(s).
■ Two-tier gold plastic pickguard (white plastic from c1963).
■ Six-saddle bridge, separate vibrato tailpiece.

375F 'second version' *1968-72 Triangle markers, three pickups, controls on body, vibrato tailpiece.*

Style Ten

■ Glued-in neck with bound fingerboard, triangle markers; 21 frets.

■ Semi-acoustic bound body with single soundhole; sunburst or natural.
■ Three pickups.
■ Five controls (two volume, two tone, one blend) and three-way selector, all on body front; side-mounted jack sockets.
■ White plastic pickguard.
■ Six-saddle bridge, separate vibrato tailpiece.

STYLE ELEVEN (1964-current)

Offset cutaways (with rounded horns providing 'sweeping crescent' profile across both) on large body

360 *1964-current Triangle markers, two pickups.*

Style Eleven

■ Glued-in neck with bound fingerboard, triangle markers; 21 frets (24 frets phased in from c1969).
■ Semi-acoustic, rear-edge-bound body with single bound soundhole; sunburst, natural or colors.
■ Two pickups.
■ Five controls (two volume, two tone, one blend) and three-way selector, all on pickguard; side-mounted jack sockets.
■ Two-tier white plastic pickguard.
■ Six-saddle bridge, separate tailpiece.

360SPC TUXEDO 6 *1987 All-white, including fingerboard.*

Style Eleven

As 360, except:
■ White neck, fingerboard and body.
■ Two-tier black plastic pickguard.
■ Black-plated hardware.

360VB See 365 listing.

360/12 *1964-current 12 strings, triangle markers, two pickups.*

Style Eleven

■ Glued-in neck with bound fingerboard, triangle markers; 21 frets (24 frets phased in from c1969); 12-string headstock.
■ Semi-acoustic, rear-edge-bound body with single bound soundhole; sunburst, natural or colors.
■ Two pickups.
■ Five controls (two volume, two tone, one blend) and three-way selector, all on pickguard; side-mounted jack sockets.
■ Two-tier white plastic pickguard.
■ Six-saddle bridge, separate tailpiece.

360/12SPC TUXEDO 12 *1987 12 strings, all-white, including fingerboard.*

Style Eleven

As 360/12, except:
■ White neck, fingerboard and body.
■ Two-tier black plastic pickguard.
■ Black-plated hardware.

365 *1964-76 and 1985-current Triangle markers, two pickups, vibrato tailpiece.*

Style Eleven

■ Glued-in neck with bound fingerboard, triangle markers; 21 frets (24 frets phased in from c1969).
■ Semi-acoustic, rear-edge-bound body with single bound soundhole; sunburst, natural or colors.
■ Two pickups.
■ Five controls (two volume, two tone, one blend) and three-way selector, all on pickguard; side-mounted jack socket.
■ Two-tier white plastic pickguard.

84

BODY STYLES
Each main model entry above includes a 'Style bar' to identify which of Rickenbacker's 15 distinctive body Styles is used. The Styles are shown in silhouette, on the right, numbered 1 to 15.

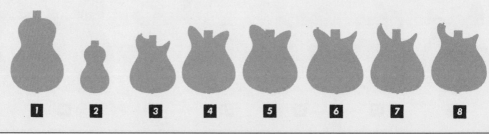

1 2 3 4 5 6 7 8

■ Six-saddle bridge, separate vibrato tailpiece.
360VB with vibrato tailpiece option (thus 365 specification) from 1985.

366/12 *1966-76 12 strings, triangle markers, two pickups, 12/6-string converter unit.*
As 360/12, except:
■ 12/6-string converter on body.

370 *1964-current Triangle markers, three pickups.*

Style Eleven

■ Glued-in neck with bound fingerboard, triangle markers; 21 frets (24 frets phased in from c1969).
■ Semi-acoustic, rear-edge-bound body with single bound soundhole; sunburst, natural or colors.
■ Three pickups.
■ Five controls (two volume, two tone, one blend) and three-way selector, all on pickguard; side-mounted jack sockets.
■ Two-tier white plastic pickguard.
■ Six-saddle bridge, separate tailpiece.
360 with third pickup option (thus 370 specification) 1986-90.

370VB See 375 listing.

370/12 *1964-current 12 strings, triangle markers, three pickups.*

Style Eleven

■ Glued-in neck with bound fingerboard, triangle markers; 21 frets (24 frets phased in from c1969); 12-string headstock.
■ Semi-acoustic, rear-edge-bound body with single bound soundhole; sunburst, natural or colors.
■ Three pickups.

■ Five controls (two volume, two tone, one blend) and three-way selector, all on pickguard; side-mounted jack sockets.
■ Two-tier white plastic pickguard.
■ Six-saddle bridge, separate tailpiece.
360/12 with third pickup option (thus 370/12 specification) 1986-90.

370/12RME1 ROGER McGUINN *1988-89 12 strings, signature on pickguard.*

Style Eleven

■ Glued-in neck with bound fingerboard, triangle markers; 21 frets.
■ Semi-acoustic, rear-edge-bound body with single bound soundhole; sunburst, natural or black.
■ Three pickups.
■ Five controls (four volume, six-way rotary tone/compression selector) and three-way selector, all on pickguard; active circuit.
■ Two-tier white plastic pickguard.
■ 12-saddle bridge, separate tailpiece.
■ Roger McGuinn signature and 'Limited Edition' on pickguard.
Limited edition of 1000. Some early examples without active circuit.

375 *1964-75 and 1985-current Triangle markers, three pickups, vibrato tailpiece.*

Style Eleven

■ Glued-in neck with bound fingerboard, triangle markers; 21 frets (24 frets phased in from c1969).
■ Semi-acoustic, rear-edge-bound body with single bound soundhole; sunburst, natural or colors.
■ Three pickups.
■ Five controls (two volume, two tone, one blend) and three-way selector, all on pickguard; side jack sockets.
■ Two-tier white plastic pickguard.

■ Six-saddle bridge, separate vibrato tailpiece.
370VB with vibrato tailpiece option or 360 with third pickup and vibrato tailpiece options (both thus 375 specification) from 1985.

STYLE TWELVE (1971-current)

Offset cutaways with rounded horns on small body

220 HAMBURG *1992-current Maple fingerboard, two controls and selector, chrome hardware.*

Style Twelve

■ Bolt-on neck with maple fingerboard, dot markers; 25in scale, 24 frets.
■ Solid body; sunburst, natural or colors.
■ Two pickups.
■ Two controls (volume, tone) and three-way selector, all on pickguard; side-mounted jack socket.
■ White plastic pickguard.
■ Six-saddle bridge/tailpiece.

230GF GLENN FREY *1992-current Signature on pickguard.*

Style Twelve

■ Bolt-on neck; dot markers; 25in scale, 24 frets.
■ Contoured solid body; all-black only.
■ Two pickups.
■ Two controls (volume, tone) and three-way selector, all on pickguard; side-mounted jack socket.
■ Silver plastic pickguard.
■ Six-saddle bridge/tailpiece.
■ Black-plated hardware.
■ Glenn Frey signature and 'Limited Edition' on pickguard.
Limited edition of 1000.

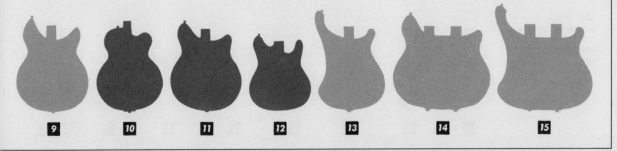

9   10   11   12   13   14   15

230 HAMBURG *1983-92 Rosewood fingerboard, four controls and selector, chrome hardware.*

Style Twelve

- Bolt-on neck; dot markers; 25in scale, 24 frets.
- Solid body; sunburst, natural, colors.
- Two pickups.
- Four controls (two volume, two tone) and three-way selector, all on body front; side-mounted jack socket.
- Six-saddle bridge/tailpiece.

250 EL DORADO *1983-92 Bound rosewood fingerboard, four controls and selector, gold hardware.*

Style Twelve

- Bolt-on neck with bound fingerboard, dot markers; 25in scale, 24 frets.
- Solid bound body; sunburst, natural or colors.
- Two pickups.
- Four controls (two volume, two tone) and three-way selector, all on body front; side-mounted jack socket.
- Six-saddle bridge/tailpiece.
- Gold-plated hardware.

260 EL DORADO *1992-current Maple fingerboard, two controls and selector, gold hardware.*

Style Twelve

- Bolt-on neck with maple fingerboard, dot markers; 25in scale, 24 frets.
- Solid bound body; sunburst, natural or colors.
- Two pickups.
- Two controls (volume, tone) and three-way selector, all on pickguard; side-mounted jack socket.
- Chrome-plated metal pickguard.

- Six-saddle bridge/tailpiece.
- Gold-plated hardware.

430 *1971-82 Rosewood fingerboard, four controls and selector, black plastic pickguard.*

Style Twelve

- Bolt-on neck; dot markers; 25in scale, 24 frets.
- Solid body; sunburst, natural, colors.
- Two pickups.
- Four controls (two volume, two tone), three-way selector and jack socket, all on pickguard.
- Black plastic pickguard.
- Six-saddle bridge/tailpiece.

STYLE THIRTEEN (1973-83)

Offset cutaways (with hooked long left horn providing 'high cresting wave' profile across both) on small body

480 *1973-83 Two pickups.*

Style Thirteen

- Bolt-on neck with bound fingerboard, dot markers; 25in scale, 24 frets.
- Solid body; sunburst, natural or colors.
- Two pickups.
- Four controls (two volume, two tone) and three-way selector, all on pickguard; side-mounted jack socket.
- White plastic pickguard.
- Six-saddle bridge, separate tailpiece.

481 *1974-83 Slanted frets, pickups and bridge.*

Style Thirteen

- Bolt-on neck with bound fingerboard, triangle markers; 25in scale, 24 slanted frets.

- Solid bound body; sunburst, natural or colors.
- Two slanted pickups.
- Four controls (two volume, two tone), three-way selector and phase mini-switch, all on pickguard; side-mounted jack socket.
- White plastic pickguard.
- Six-saddle slanted bridge, separate tailpiece.

483 *1980-83 Three pickups.*

Style Thirteen

- Bolt-on neck with bound fingerboard, dot markers; 25in scale, 24 frets.
- Solid body; sunburst, natural or colors.
- Three pickups.
- Four controls (two volume, two tone) and three-way selector, all on pickguard; side-mounted jack socket.
- White plastic pickguard.
- Six-saddle bridge, separate tailpiece.

STYLE FOURTEEN (1975-92)

Offset cutaways with rounded horns on double neck large body

362/12 *1975-92 12 and six-string necks.*

Style Fourteen

- Glued-in necks with bound fingerboards, triangle markers; 24 frets per neck.
- Semi-acoustic bound body with single bound soundhole; sunburst, natural or colors.
- Two pickups per neck.
- Five controls (two volume, two tone, one blend) and two three-way selectors, all on pickguard; side-mounted jack sockets.

86

BODY STYLES
Each main model entry above includes a 'Style bar' to identify which of Rickenbacker's 15 distinctive body Styles is used. The Styles are shown in silhouette, on the right, numbered 1 to 15.

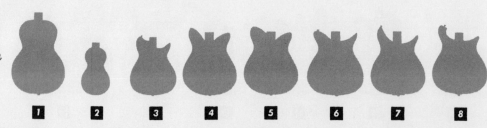

1   2   3   4   5   6   7   8

▌White plastic pickguard.
▌Six saddle bridge, separate tailpiece per neck.

STYLE FIFTEEN (1975-92)

Offset cutaways with hooked long left horn on double neck large body

4080 *1975-92 Four-string bass and six-string necks.*

Style Fifteen

▌Bolt-on necks with bound fingerboards, triangle markers; 20 frets on bass neck, 24 frets on guitar neck.
▌Solid bound body; sunburst, natural or colors.
▌Two pickups per neck.
▌Five controls (two volume, two tone, one blend) and two three-way selectors, all on pickguard; side-mounted jack sockets.
▌Black plastic pickguard.
▌Four-saddle bridge/tailpiece for bass neck; six-saddle bridge, separate tailpiece for guitar neck.

4080/12 *1977-92 Four-string bass and 12-string necks.*

Style Fifteen

▌Bolt-on necks with bound fingerboards, triangle markers; 20 frets on bass neck, 24 frets on 12-string neck.
▌Solid bound body; sunburst, natural or colors.
▌Two pickups per neck.
▌Five controls (two volume, two tone, one blend) and two three-way selectors, all on pickguard; side-mounted jack sockets.

▌Black plastic pickguard.
▌Four-saddle bridge/tailpiece for bass neck; six-saddle bridge, separate tailpiece for 12-string neck.

MISCELLANEOUS MAKES AND MODELS

Rickenbacker manufactured some guitars which did not carry the company name.

ASTRO AS-51 *(1963-64) Unique shape solid body, with offset dot markers and one pickup, marketed as a 'kit of parts' guitar.*

CONTELLO 425 *(1962) Based on the Rickenbacker 425 with 'Style 8' body shape, but with Contello logo on headstock.*

ELECTRO ES-16 *(1964-71) Based on the Rickenbacker Model 1000 with 'Style 6' body shape, but pickup located mid-way between neck and bridge. Sold as part of a set with companion amplifier.*

ELECTRO ES-17 *(1964-75) Based on the Rickenbacker 425 with 'Style 8' body shape, but pickup located mid-way between neck and bridge. Sold as part of a set with companion amplifier.*

RYDER 425 *(1963) Based on the Rickenbacker 425 with 'Style 8' body shape, but with Ryder logo on headstock.*

87

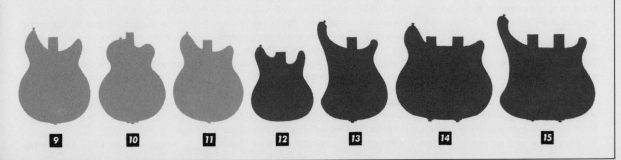

9   10   11   12   13   14   15

In addition to the Reference Listing, the following information may be of assistance.

MODEL NUMBERS & NAMES

Any designation, whether number or name, is usually conspicuous by its absence from Rickenbacker's guitars, but there are exceptions: some examples do have the model number on the truss-rod cover. Otherwise all Rickenbacker titles, as used in this book, are dependent on those shown in company literature and pricelists. These display occasional lapses in consistency, content and the compiler's descriptive powers.

PRODUCTION DATES

Rickenbacker pricelists can sometimes indicate erratic production of certain models – some seemingly ceasing only to re-appear later, and not always in the same guise. In reality production was more constant, with longevity assured by the provision of various Special Order options (see next entry).

Thanks to Rickenbacker's numbering system, a model officially no longer offered could still be obtained as a special order by up-grading a still-listed standard version, adding for example a third pickup and/or vibrato tailpiece. The company pricelists vary in their approach to these aspects, either continuing to show the model proper, or else indicating availability only by recourse to the option method.

Where applicable we have chosen to combine the officially listed model and the special order version under one overall production span. This naturally results in extended and continuous periods of availability, which makes things easier to understand and we feel more accurately reflects Rickenbacker's production policy.

SPECIAL ORDER OPTIONS

Rickenbacker has provided quite a varied menu of optional features available on a special order basis.

The left-handed version is an obvious alternative, but right-handed stringing on a lefty is a much more unusual variation that is very rarely encountered.

Slant Frets were intended to offer improved comfort and playability, but the unusual visuals were enough to guarantee little demand.

Various cosmetic choices have been offered, such as custom colors and black-and-white checkered body binding. Custom Trim described reversed color choices of body binding and plastic components – black instead of standard white, or white instead of standard black.

Different pickups have come in the form of medium, high and very high gain units, more recently custom or vintage types.

The additional third pickup option has appeared at various times, available on suitable models. This option is usually offered when the three-pickup versions are not officially listed.

A similar situation exists with the Vintage RIC vibrato tailpiece, which is the original Ac'cent unit revived. Guitars thus optionally equipped are normally offered when the appropriate official versions are not shown to be available.

Latest option is the choice of a 'high performance vibrato system' for the 650 and 200 series solids.

CATALOGS & PRICELISTS

Thanks to Rickenbacker's archive we had access to a complete run of catalogs and pricelists. Those that are shown or referred to directly in this book are listed in the general index (pages 92-95).

PICKGUARDS

In late 1958 Rickenbacker replaced the single pickguard used on some models with a novel and distinctive two-piece type. This new version stylishly combined a large pickguard base with a separate small upper section, the latter being raised on three spacers thus becoming a pickguard. In the interests of brevity, this pairing is described as a 'two-tier' pickguard throughout this book.

SOUNDHOLES

Most of the semi-acoustic models come with an appropriate single soundhole, although it has sometimes been absent from the short-scale 310/320 series. Styling of the soundhole varies: it is either a scimitar-like 'slash' or the more traditional 'f' shape. The latter was one of the features specified by UK importers Rose-Morris for the 1960s export versions.

SHIPPING TOTALS

Rickenbacker confirms that shipping totals previously published elsewhere are far from accurate. The figures contained therein were compiled from only a small selection of invoice documentation, with consequent errors in yearly output, and quantities significantly less than the actual numbers produced.

DATING RICKENBACKER GUITARS

Ascertaining the age of an instrument is a priority for most owners. While the personal satisfaction gained from accurately deducing such an important piece of information is obvious, all too often age can have a direct bearing on value, particularly regarding those examples deemed to be in the 'vintage' bracket. The Rickenbacker company has been responsible for a selection of models that have since assumed collectible status, and as always an association with famous names is the most influential factor in determining the chosen few.

Rickenbackers, like the guitars from virtually any manufacturer, are difficult to date with scientific precision, and an approximate age should be considered a safe ideal. Serial numbers can provide an indicator as to production period, if not always the exact year. The system employed by Rickenbacker since 1960 is generally regarded to be more accurate than most, suggesting that the company applied the numbers with more diligence and consistency than many of their contemporaries. This is fortunate as a number of models, such as various vintage reissues, do look very similar and the serial number must then play a major role in identifying the true production period.

However, prior to 1960 things were

not so straightforward. Many 1930s and 1940s models did not come with serial numbers, so no help is forthcoming from this quarter to date such oldies. Into the 1950s and the situation improves somewhat. The assorted Combos and Models used numbers that comprised anything from four to seven characters. Of these the first, second or third was a letter, and the following numeral denotes the production year, being a 1950s multiple.

For example: 6C7161 – the seven indicates 1957.

85C7113 – again the seven indicates 1957.

Unfortunately this method was not consistently employed, so there are exceptions. Also it was not allocated to the semi-acoustics of the same period, which bear serial numbers that have little coherence and are thus of no real relevance to dating.

In late 1960 Rickenbacker instituted a new system which was to be applied with seemingly logical consistency over the next 26 years. The revised scheme comprised two, three or four-digit numbers, all plus a two-letter coded prefix. The first letter indicates the year, while the second provides the month. The table below shows a complete listing of both letter codes.

The final year of the letter sequence was 1986, so Rickenbacker had to come up with an all-new method for the following year. Again the company opted to use a coded format, and accordingly the new system was

introduced in 1987. This employed two, three or four digits as before, but this time with a prefix comprising a letter and a number. The former denotes the month, with the coding unchanged from the previous scheme, while the single number signifies the year. Details of this new arrangement are as follows.

Number in prefix = Year
0 – 1987
1 – 1988
2 – 1989
3 – 1990
4 – 1991
5 – 1992
6 – 1993
7 – 1994
8 – 1995
9 – 1996

For example: H5 5944 – the prefix denotes August 1992.

K6 5497 – here it signifies November 1993.

Rickenbacker serial numbers are found either stamped on the bridge, neckplate or more commonly on the jackplate. The fact that the latter is readily removable means that exchange for a more valuable, earlier example is equally easy. For this reason it is best to use the serial number in conjunction with other clues. Rickenbacker did make some across-the-board changes to components and cosmetics, many occurring in the mid 1960s, and these serve as useful pointers when trying to determine the age of an instrument.

CONTROLS & KNOBS

A distinctive modification took place in the Rickenbacker line between 1961 and 1963. The standard two-volume, two-tone layout was augmented by a fifth control, identified by a smaller knob, and its 'blend' function provided additional preset volume and tone facilities (see pages 32/33).

The control knobs too underwent some changes at this time, the large 'oven' type of the 1950s being replaced by smaller black varieties.

An additional bonus was Rick-O-Sound pseudo-stereo, with twin output jack sockets. It was introduced as a standard feature on the deluxe models from 1960.

PLASTIC PARTS

Another change occurred during the 1962-63 period when the company decided to switch to white plastic for pickguards and truss-rod covers, replacing the gold finished variety used previously.

TAILPIECE

The original and somewhat austere flat 'trapeze' tailpiece was supplanted during 1963 on most models by the more visual 'R' variety.

CONTROL POT CODES

The metal casings of many American-made control potentiometers (usually called 'pots') are stamped with code numbers which include date information, and these can therefore provide useful confirmation of an instrument's age. However, be aware that pots were not always used immediately, and also that they may have been replaced, factors which could cause contradiction and confusion. The code comprises six or seven numbers. Of these the first three identify the manufacturer and can be disregarded, while the final two indicate the week of the production year. In a six-figure code the fourth number indicates the last digit of the appropriate year during the 1950s period, i.e. 195?. In a seven figure code, the fourth and fifth numbers show the last two digits of any year thereafter.

89

First letter = Year	First letter = Year	Second letter = Month
A – 1961	N – 1974	A – January
B – 1962	O – 1975	B – February
C – 1963	P – 1976	C – March
D – 1964	Q – 1977	D – April
E – 1965	R – 1978	E – May
F – 1966	S – 1979	F – June
G – 1967	T – 1980	G – July
H – 1968	U – 1981	H – August
I – 1969	V – 1982	I/J – September
J – 1960/70	W – 1983	J/K – October
K – 1971	X – 1984	K/L – November
L – 1972	Y – 1985	L/M – December
M – 1973	Z – 1986	

For example: AA 47 – the prefix indicates 1961, January

MODELS & YEARS

This listing shows the models produced by Rickenbacker, in chronological order of introduction. The number in the box refers to the body shape.

Box	Model	Years
1	Electro Spanish (wood body)	1932-35
1	Ken Roberts	1935-40
2	Electro Spanish (Bakelite body)	1935-42
2	Vibrola Spanish (Bakelite body)	1937-42
1	S-59	1940-42
1	Spanish (SP)	1946-50
3	Combo 600	1954-59
3	Combo 800	1954-59
4	Combo 400	1956-57
4	Combo 450	1957
5	Model 900	1957
5	Model 950	1957
4	Model 1000	1957
6	Combo 400	1957-58
6	Combo 450	1957-58
6	Model 900	1957-71
6	Model 950	1957-71
6	Model 1000	1957-71
7	Combo 650	1957-59
7	Combo 850	1957-59
7	310	1958-71, 1981-84
7	315	1958-75
7	320	1958-75
7	325	1958-75, 1985-92
9	330	1958-current
9	335	1958-77, 1985-current
9	340	1958-current
9	345	1958-75, 1985-current
9	360	1958-current
9	365	1958-76, 1985-current
9	370	1958-current
9	375	1958-74, 1985-current
9	381	1958-63, 1969-74
8	425	1958-72
8	450	1958-85
10	330F	1959-67
10	340F	1959-67
10	335F	1959-67
10	345F	1959-67
10	360F	1959-67, 1968-72
10	365F	1959-67, 1968-72
10	370F	1959-67, 1968-72
10	375F	1959-67, 1968-72
8	460	1961-85
8	615	1962-74, 1985-current
8	625	1962-74, 1985-current
9	360/12	1964-current
9	370/12	1964-current
11	370/12	1964-current
8	450/12	1964-85
11	360	1964-current
11	365	1964-76, 1985-current
11	370	1964-current
11	375	1964-75, 1985-current
11	360/12	1964-current
9	330/12	1965-current

	Model	Years		Model	Years
8	420	1965-83	7	325/12	1985-86
9	336/12 'Convertible'	1966-76	8	610	1985-current
11	366/12 'Convertible'	1966-76	11	360SPC Tuxedo 6	1987
8	456/12 'Convertible'	1966-75	11	360/12SPC Tuxedo 12	1987
9	381/12	1969-74	9	381V69	1987-current
9	331 'Light Show'	1970-76	9	1997	1987-current
9	331/12 'Light Show'	1970-75	9	1997VB	1987-current
12	430	1971-82	9	1998PT Pete Townshend	1987-88
8	900	1971-79	8	610/12	1988 current
8	950	1971-79	11	370/12RME1 Roger McGuinn	1988-89
10	360/12F	1973-80	7	350SH Susanna Hoffs	1988-90
13	480	1973-83	9	381JK John Kay	1988-current
13	481 'Slanted frets'	1974-83	9	381/12V69	1988-current
8	620	1974-current	7	325JL John Lennon	1989-93
14	362/12 '12/6 Double Neck'	1975-92	7	355JL John Lennon	1989-93
15	4080 '4/6 Double Neck'	1975-92	7	355JLVB John Lennon	1989-93
15	4080/12 '4/12 Double Neck'	1977-92	7	355/12JL John Lennon	1989-93
9	340/12	1980-current	9	360V64	1991-current
13	483	1980-83	8	660/12TP Tom Petty	1991-current
8	620/12	1981-current	8	650E Excalibur	1991-current
12	230 Hamburg	1983-92	12	220 Hamburg	1992-current
12	250 El Dorado	1983-92	12	230GF Glenn Frey	1992-current
7	320B	1983-84	12	260 El Dorado	1992-current
7	325B	1983-84	9	1997SPC	1992-current
9	360/12B WB	1983-84	8	650A Atlantis	1992-current
7	350 Liverpool	1983-current	8	650D Dakota	1993-current
7	355 Liverpool Plus	1983-current	8	650S Sierra	1993-current
7	325V59	1984-current	8	650C Colorado	1993-current
7	325V63	1984-current	7	350V63	1994-current
9	360/12V64	1984-current	7	350/12V63	1994-current

92

93

94

95

OWNERS' CREDITS

Guitars photographed came from the following individuals' collections, and we are most grateful for their help.

The owners are listed here in the alphabetical order of the code used to identify their guitars in the Key to Guitar Photographs below.

AM Albert Molinaro (Guitars R Us); **AR** Alan Rogan; **JN** John Nelson; **KC** Keith Clark (Voltage); **MA** Macari's Musical Instruments; **MP** Matt Preble; **NR** Nick Rowlands; **PQ** Pat Quilter; **RI** Rickenbacker International Corporation; **SB** Steve Boyer; **SJ** Scott Jennings; **SR** Scott Jennings/Route 66; **YO** Yoko Ono; **ZZ** Zeke Zirngiebel.

Please note that the 460 pictured across pages 22/23 was stolen just after we photographed it. It has serial number AJ653. If you have any information concerning its whereabouts, please contact the publishers.

KEY TO GUITAR PHOTOGRAPHS

The following key is designed to identify who owned which guitars when they were photographed for the book. After the relevant page number we list the model followed by its owner's initials in bold letters (check the Owners' Credits above). For example, `2/3: 1959 360 **SR**' means that the 1959 360 guitar shown across pages 2 and 3 was owned by Scott Jennings/Route 66.

Jacket front: 1968 360 **MP**, 1992 330/12 **MA**. *2/3:* 1959 360 **SR**. *2:* 1964 Model 1000 **RI**. *6:* 365 **MP**; Frying Pan **RI**. *10/11:* Electro Spanish **PQ**. *10:* Spanish (SP) **RI**. *11:* Combo 800 **JN**; Combo 600 blond **RI**; Combo 600 turquoise blue **RI**. *14/15:* Combo 450 **RI**; Model 1000 **SR**. *15:* Model 1000 **RI**; Combo 400 **KC**. *18:* Combo 850 **RI**; 325S/1996 **NR**. *19:* all **YO**. *22/23:* 460 **AM**; 615 **RI**. *23:* 450-12 **SR**; detail 456/12 **RI**; 625 **RI**. *26:* both **RI**. *27:* 460 **SR**; 650 Sierra **RI**. *30/31:* 330 **RI**; 360 **SR**. *31:* 335S/1997 **SR**; 1998PT **RI**; 360 **AM**. *34:* 336/12 **RI**; 330-12S/1993 **AR**; 360-12V64 **RI**. *35:* both **RI**. *38/39:* all **RI**. *42/43:* all **RI**. *46:* 360 **RI**; 360SF **SB**. *47:* 375 (& back) **SB**; 360 **RI**. *50/51:* 360/12 leftie **ZZ**; 370-12RM **RI**. *50:* 360-12SPC **RI**. *51:* 360-12 **RI**. *54/55:* all **RI**. *58/59:* both **RI**. *62:* Browne **RI**; 335 **SJ**. *63:* 335 experiment **RI**; first 12-string **SJ**; Astro **RI**; System 490 **RI**. *Jacket back:* 1964 325S/1996 **NR**.

All guitar photography is by Nigel Bradley, of Visuel 7. There are a few exceptions: the Lennon guitars on page 19 come from the Lenono Photo Archive; the 362/12 on page 59 comes from Rickenbacker's picture archive; and the first 12-string, shown on page 63, was snapped by Jeff Veitch. Thanks be to all.

MEMORABILIA

MEMORABILIA including catalogs, brochures, magazines and photographs came from the collections of Tony Bacon, Paul Day, Rickenbacker International Corporation, and Rickenbacker UK. Each item was lovingly photographed by Nigel Bradley and Will Taylor of Visuel 7. The shot of happy Pete Townshend in front of the smashed guitars (page 31) is reproduced by kind permission of the photographer, Colin Jones.

INTERVIEWS

We are very grateful to the many individuals who consented to be interviewed for this book. Unsourced quotations are from original interviews conducted specially by Tony Bacon with: Suzi Arden (March 1994); Dick Burke (November 1993, March 1994); Derek Davis (March 1994); FC Hall (November 1993); John Hall (November 1993, March 1994); Chris Huston (March 1994); Ted McCarty (October 1992); Roger McGuinn (March 1994); Don Randall (February 1992); and Joe Talbot (March 1994). ▌ The quotations from Peter Buck, George Harrison, Johnny Marr, Tom Petty, Pete Townshend and Paul Weller come from a BBC Radio 1 program *A Concise History Of The Frying Pan* (presented by Mike Read, produced by Mark Radcliffe and first broadcast in 1987). ▌ The quotation by David Crosby comes from *Timeless Flight* (Johnny Rogan); the quotation on page 5 by Johnny Marr comes from *Guitar Player* and by George Harrison from *Beat Monthly*. The sources of other previously published quotations are given where they occur in the text. ▌ Brian Carman worked for Rickenbacker from 1965 to 1974 and from 1984 to October 1993; as a result of his recent and sudden departure from the company, he decided not to be interviewed for this book.

IN ADDITION

IN ADDITION to those named above in OWNERS' CREDITS and in INTERVIEWS we would like to thank: Alf Bicknell; Julie Bowie; Walter Carter; Lloyd Chiate (Voltage); Jim Cooper; Jane, Sarah & Simon Day; André Duchossoir; Linda Garson (Rickenbacker UK); Nick Hall (*The Observer*); Larry Henrickson (Ax-In-Hand); Steve Jolly (Holiday Music); Colin Jones; Helmuth Lemme; Jon Lewin (*Making Music*); Dave Liddle (Q7); Karla Merrifeld (Lenono Photo Archive); Ian Purser; Heinz Rebellius (Musik Produktiv); Martin Scott (MPL); Peter S Shukat (Shukat Arrow Hafer & Weber); Jeff Simpson (BBC Radio 1); Kate Smith (Handmade Films); Trevor Smith (Rickenbacker UK); Steve Soest

(Soest Guitar Repair); Toshio Sogabe (Rick's International Corp, Japan).

VERY SPECIAL THANKS

VERY SPECIAL THANKS to John Hall at Rickenbacker International Corporation for his generous hospitality, for allowing us to rummage freely through his (abundant) filing cabinets, and for letting us dismantle, strum and photograph his guitar collection. If only other guitar companies were so aware of their own history... We would also like to thank the many other people at Rickenbacker who made our stay so enjoyable and productive, especially Shirley Swanson, Cindalee Hall, FC Hall, and Dick Burke.

SPECIAL THANKS

SPECIAL THANKS to Scott Jennings of Route 66 for lining up some wonderful instruments in front of Nigel The Lens, and for sharing with us his 13-year knowledge of Rickenbackers and Rickenbacker people.

BIBLIOGRAPHY

Tony Bacon & Paul Day *The Fender Book* (Miller Freeman 1992), *The Gibson Les Paul Book* (Miller Freeman 1993), *The Ultimate Guitar Book* (Knopf 1991), *The Guru's Guitar Guide* (Making Music 1990/1992); Harry Benson *The Beatles In The Beginning* (Mainstream 1993); *Beat Instrumental* magazine; *Beat Monthly* magazine; Bob Brozman *The History & Artistry Of National Resonator Instruments* (Centerstream 1993); Robert & Celia Dearling *Guinness Book Of Recorded Sound* (Guinness 1984); André Duchossoir *Gibson Electrics – The Classic Years* (Hal Leonard 1994); George Gruhn & Walter Carter *Gruhn's Guide To Vintage Guitars* (GPI 1991); *Guitar Digest* magazine; *The Guitar Magazine*; *Guitar Player* magazine; *Guitar World* magazine; *Guitarist* magazine; Colin Larkin (editor) *The Guinness Encyclopedia Of Popular Music* (Guinness 1992); Mark Lewisohn *The Complete Beatles Recording Sessions* (Hamlyn 1988), *The Complete Beatles Chronicle* (Pyramid 1992); *Making Music* magazine; *Music Trades* magazine; *Observer Sunday Magazine*; *One Two Testing* magazine; Johnny Rogan *Timeless Flight* (Square One 1990); Norbert Schnepel & Helmuth Lemme *Elektro-Gitarren Made In Germany* English translation JP Klink (Musik-Verlag Schnepel-Lemme 1988); Richard Smith *The Complete History Of Rickenbacker Guitars* (Centerstream 1987); Andrew Solt & Sam Egan *Imagine John Lennon* (Bloomsbury 1988); *20th Century Guitar* magazine; Paul Trynka (editor) *The Electric Guitar* (Virgin 1993); *Vintage Gallery* magazine; *Vintage Guitar* magazine.